**New Directions for
Institutional Research**

Paul D. Umbach
EDITOR-IN-CHIEF

J. Fredericks Volkwein
ASSOCIATE EDITOR

M000099431

Multilevel Modeling Techniques and Applications in Institutional Research

Joe L. Lott, II
James S. Antony
EDITORS

Number 154 • Summer 2012
Jossey-Bass
San Francisco

MULTILEVEL MODELING TECHNIQUES AND APPLICATIONS IN INSTITUTIONAL RESEARCH
Joe L. Lott, II and James S. Antony (eds.)
New Directions for Institutional Research, no. 154
Paul D. Umbach, Editor-in-Chief

Copyright © 2012 Wiley Periodicals, Inc., A Wiley Company

All rights reserved. No part of this publication may be reproduced in any form or by any means, except as permitted under section 107 or 108 of the 1976 United States Copyright Act, without either the prior written permission of the publisher or authorization through the Copyright Clearance Center, 222 Rosewood Drive, Danvers, MA 01923; (978) 750-8400; fax (978) 646-8600. The code and copyright notice appearing at the bottom of the first page of an article in this journal indicate the copyright holder's consent that copies may be made for personal or internal use, or for personal or internal use of specific clients, on the condition that the copier pay for copying beyond that permitted by law. This consent does not extend to other kinds of copying, such as copying for general distribution, for advertising or promotional purposes, for creating collective works, or for resale. Such permission requests and other permission inquiries should be addressed to the Permissions Department, c/o John Wiley & Sons, Inc., 111 River St., Hoboken, NJ 07030; (201) 748-8789, fax (201) 748-6326, http://www.wiley.com/go/permissions.

NEW DIRECTIONS FOR INSTITUTIONAL RESEARCH (ISSN 0271-0579, electronic ISSN 1536-075X) is part of The Jossey-Bass Higher and Adult Education Series and is published quarterly by Wiley Subscription Services, Inc., A Wiley Company, at Jossey-Bass, One Montgomery Street, Suite 1200, San Francisco, California 94104-4594 (publication number USPS 098-830). Periodicals Postage Paid at San Francisco, California, and at additional mailing offices. POSTMASTER: Send address changes to New Directions for Institutional Research, Jossey-Bass, One Montgomery Street, Suite 1200, San Francisco, California 94104-4594.

SUBSCRIPTIONS cost $109 for individuals and $297 for institutions, agencies, and libraries in the United States. See order form at end of book.

EDITORIAL CORRESPONDENCE should be sent to Paul D. Umbach, Leadership, Policy and Adult and Higher Education, North Carolina State University, Poe 300, Box 7801, Raleigh, NC 27695-7801.

New Directions for Institutional Research is indexed in Academic Search (EBSCO), Academic Search Elite (EBSCO), Academic Search Premier (EBSCO), CIJE: Current Index to Journals in Education (ERIC), Contents Pages in Education (T&F), EBSCO Professional Development Collection (EBSCO), Educational Research Abstracts Online (T&F), ERIC Database (Education Resources Information Center), Higher Education Abstracts (Claremont Graduate University), Multicultural Education Abstracts (T&F), Sociology of Education Abstracts (T&F).

Microfilm copies of issues and chapters are available in 16mm and 35mm, as well as microfiche in 105mm, through University Microfilms, Inc., 300 North Zeeb Road, Ann Arbor, Michigan 48106-1346.

www.josseybass.com

THE ASSOCIATION FOR INSTITUTIONAL RESEARCH was created in 1966 to benefit, assist, and advance research leading to improved understanding, planning, and operation of institutions of higher education. Publication policy is set by its Publications Committee.

PUBLICATIONS COMMITTEE

Gary R. Pike (Chair)	Indiana University–Purdue University Indianapolis
Gloria Crisp	University of Texas at San Antonio
Paul Duby	Northern Michigan University
James Hearn	University of Georgia
Terry T. Ishitani	University of Memphis
Jan W. Lyddon	San Jacinto Community College
John R. Ryan	The Ohio State University

EX-OFFICIO MEMBERS OF THE PUBLICATIONS COMMITTEE

John Muffo (Editor, Assessment in the Disciplines), Ohio Board of Regents
John C. Smart (Editor, Research in Higher Education), University of Memphis
Richard D. Howard (Editor, Resources in Institutional Research), University of
    Minnesota
Paul D. Umbach (Editor, New Directions for Institutional Research),
    North Carolina State University
Marne K. Einarson (Editor, AIR Electronic Newsletter), Cornell University
Gerald W. McLaughlin (Editor, AIR Professional File/IR Applications), DePaul
    University
Richard J. Kroc II (Chair, Forum Publications Committee), University of
    Arizona
Sharron L. Ronco (Chair, Best Visual Presentation Committee), Florida Atlantic
    University
Randy Swing (Staff Liaison)

For information about the Association for Institutional Research, write to the following address:

AIR Executive Office
1435 E. Piedmont Drive
Suite 211
Tallahassee, FL 32308-7955

(850) 385-4155

air@mailer.fsu.edu
http://airweb.org

CONTENTS

EDITORS' NOTES

Many colleges and universities currently face mounting pressure to shrink their budgets and maximize resources on one hand, and they are expected to maintain and even increase their institutional profile on the other hand. Institutional research (IR) offices play central roles in addressing this rather dubious task through their multidimensional roles associated with institutional planning and decision making. Terenzini (1999) describes these roles in three tiers that promote the position of IR as organizational intelligence: (1) technical and analytical intelligence—factual knowledge or information, and analytical and methodological skills; (2) issues intelligence—substantive problems on which technical and analytical intelligence is brought to bear; and (3) contextual intelligence—understanding the culture of higher education and the particular campus where the researcher works. The functions associated with these IR roles are carried out by forging connections among institutional research, planning and budgeting, and assessment, effectiveness, and accreditation; or, as Volkwein (2008) calls them, the golden triangle of IR. The technical and analytical tier, which requires the most basic knowledge of statistics foundational to all practitioners in IR, is one of the most important functions.

Technical and analytical tools are increasing at a rapid pace, and a better understanding of them allows the IR practitioner to conduct research and shape institutional policy using cutting-edge technologies and methodologies. Delaney's (1997) study of 243 New England colleges and universities found that many IR practitioners have limited methodological and technical expertise. Volkwein (2008) reminds us that "the primary role of IR has changed over time from emphasizing and requiring primarily descriptive statistics, fact books, and reporting to more analysis and evaluation, both quantitative and qualitative" (p. 8). It is important for IR practitioners to be on the cutting edge of research methodologies, particularly those that inform multivariate models. Multivariate models allow the IR practitioner to understand how the outcome of interest is affected by more than one variable.

Multilevel modeling is an increasingly popular multivariate technique. It is also referred to as hierarchical linear modeling (HLM), mixed-effects modeling, random-effects modeling, and covariance component modeling (Raudenbush and Bryk, 2002). Increasingly, IR practitioners are informing institutional decisions based on results from their multivariate analyses, which often come from nested data. Nested data are cases where

NEW DIRECTIONS FOR INSTITUTIONAL RESEARCH, no. 154, Summer 2012 © Wiley Periodicals, Inc.
Published online in Wiley Online Library (wileyonlinelibrary.com) • DOI: 10.1002/ir.20010

lower-level units are located within one or more higher-level units. Common examples from data for many IR practitioners include students nested within institutions, students nested within majors or classes, and faculty nested within departments. HLM provides a class of models that take into account the hierarchical, or nested, structure of data and makes it possible to incorporate variables from all levels and examine how the variability in the outcome can be explained within and between nests, or clusters (Raudenbush and Bryk, 2002).

Countless studies have used institutional data to estimate multivariate models with student and faculty outcomes. Regarding student outcomes, most multi-institutional college impact studies have relied on ordinary least squares (OLS) regression (Astin and Denson, 2009). Since the 1960s, many studies have relied on OLS regression because it became increasingly sophisticated and complex, and developments in SPSS made it more efficient by giving users options that showed direct and indirect paths to the dependent variable and how each indirect path had been mediated by the action of other intervening variables (Astin and Denson, 2009). The advent and popularity of multilevel techniques provided insight into the limitations of OLS approaches; mainly in the presence of nested data, OLS techniques violate the assumption of independence that leads to imprecise parameter estimates and loss of statistical power, and increases the likelihood of rejecting a true null hypothesis (Snijders and Bosker, 1999; Raudenbush and Bryk, 2002). In addition, Astin and Denson (2009) observed that "increasing numbers of editorial reviewers for scholar journals are now routinely recommending that HLM rather than OLS regression be used whenever a study using individual and institutional data is submitted" (p. 365). Although they note the circumstances under which OLS could be applicable, they underscore the value of using HLM approaches where applicable. It is imperative that IR practitioners understand the nature of multimodeling techniques so they can properly model their nested and sometimes dependent data structures. Many times institutional decisions are based on feedback and analyses from IR practitioners, and multilevel modeling is one tool that will lead to more efficient estimations and enhance the ability to better understand complex relationships with nested data.

Chapters in this volume illustrate both the theoretical and practical information about using multilevel modeling in IR. Chapter 1 introduces the fundamental concepts of hierarchy and its statistical treatment in institutional research settings. This chapter also provides an overview and highlights the advantages of HLM and sets the stage for chapters that follow. By briefly discussing historical approaches to analyzing data with multilevel structures, the chapter provides a foundation to understand the nature and the kinds of variability present in data.

Chapter 2 builds on Chapter 1 by providing a conceptual, nontechnical overview of estimation and model fit issues in multilevel modeling. Being very didactic in their approach, the authors discuss the rationale for using maximum likelihood estimation in multilevel modeling and explain the approach for understanding the reliability of parameter estimates with empirical Bayes estimation. This chapter also introduces hypothesis testing in multilevel modeling and several model index comparison approaches to evaluate the goodness of fit where the researcher compares competing models and the estimation procedures to consider in these model comparisons. Although the chapter is more conceptual than technical, the authors provide many resources for follow-up discussions on concepts illuminated in the chapter.

Chapter 3 highlights the various data sources that lend themselves to multilevel modeling and IR, including a discussion about public, private, and institutional data. This chapter also provides information about some matters that should be taken into account when working with large-scale data sets. Importantly, the authors discuss the benefits and challenges of some software packages commonly used to estimate multilevel models. They also provide a brief word on missing data and how the software packages accommodate missing data.

Chapter 4 discusses multilevel models for binary outcomes, which is becoming increasingly utilized in social science research. This chapter focuses on methods for binary and binomial data and models for categorical data analysis that are adapted to both multilevel and mixed modeling frameworks using generalized linear mixed modeling. To make the text more concrete, the author provides two examples of multilevel modeling with categorical outcomes. One study evaluates the probability of placement into postdoctoral training based on a data set consisting of 40 Ph.D.-granting institutions. The second example uses data from 3,600 graduate students who entered various Ph.D. programs to examine the probability of program dropout for students who entered science, technology, engineering, and math programs.

Chapter 5 provides one example of how cross-classified random effects modeling can be used to assess faculty gender pay differentials in higher education and how those results can be used to help inform policy at the institutional level. Using data collected from the 2004 National Study of Postsecondary Faculty, this chapter provides a good example of an HLM study that has a complex data structure. Results from this chapter provide guidance for understanding macro-level issues and trends and examining institutional policies using HLM techniques.

Chapter 6 provides an example of a study that uses institutional data and multilevel modeling to examine the effects that high school academic performance and first-year college students' academic persistence have on the likelihood to participate in learning communities. This chapter takes the reader through the multilevel model building process that evolved from preliminary binomial logistic regression models. It also provides recommendations that promote retention efforts for certain student groups based on results from their multilevel models.

The final chapter, Chapter 7, provides a fuller conversation about presenting results. This chapter is an appropriate end to the volume because it provides strategies for presenting complex multilevel data and statistical results to institutional and higher education decision makers. Using two examples of research studies, one predicting first-year college grade point average and the other perception of gains in critical thinking of college seniors, this chapter shows how to communicate results to audiences that may not have prior exposure to statistical models and results from multilevel data. In addition, the chapter gives examples of how charts and graphs can be useful in communicating results.

Joe L. Lott, II
James S. Antony
Editors

References

Astin, A. W., and Denson, N. "Multi-Campus Studies of College Impact: Which Statistical Method Is Appropriate." *Research in Higher Education*, 2009, *50*, 354–367.

Delaney, A. M. "The Role of Institutional Research in Higher Education: Enabling Researchers to Meet New Challenges." *Research in Higher Education*, 1997, *38*(1), 1–16.

Raudenbush, S. W., and Bryk, A. S. *Hierarchical Linear Models: Applications and Data Analysts.* (2nd ed.). Thousand Oaks, Calif.: Sage Publications, 2002.

Snijders, T., and Bosker, R. *Multilevel Analysis.* Thousand Oaks, Calif.: Sage Publications, 1999.

Terenzini, P. T. "On the Nature of Institutional Research and the Knowledge and Skills It Requires." In J. F. Volkwein (ed.), *What Is Institutional Research All About? A Critical and Comprehensive Assessment of the Profession.* New Directions for Institutional Research, no. 104. San Francisco: Jossey-Bass, 1999.

Volkwein, J. F. "The Foundations and Evolution of Institutional Research." In D. G. Terkla (ed.), *More Than Just Data.* New Directions for Higher Education, no. 141. San Francisco: Jossey-Bass, 2008.

1

This chapter provides an introduction to multilevel modeling, including the impact of clustering and the intraclass correlation coefficient. Prototypical research questions in institutional research are examined, and an example is provided to illustrate the application and interpretation of multilevel models.

Hierarchical Data Structures, Institutional Research, and Multilevel Modeling

Ann A. O'Connell, Sandra J. Reed

Introduction

Multilevel modeling (MLM), also referred to as hierarchical linear modeling (HLM) or mixed models, provides a powerful analytical framework through which to study colleges and universities and their impact on students. Due to the natural hierarchical structure of data obtained from students or faculty in colleges and universities, MLM offers many advantages to analysts and policy makers involved in institutional research (IR). This chapter introduces fundamental concepts of hierarchy and its statistical treatment specifically for data structures occurring in IR settings. Our goal is to provide an overview of HLM and set the stage for the chapters that follow as well as highlight the particular advantages of HLM for those involved in IR.

IR professionals routinely encounter the kinds of clustered or nested data structures for which HLM is uniquely suited. Cross-sectional studies of students nested within classes or courses, classes nested within departments or schools, faculty within departments, athletes within sport designations within departments or schools—each of these settings describes lower-level individuals (that is, students or faculty) nested or clustered within one or more higher-level contexts or groups (that is, within classes or within departments). In such cases, the variability in lower-level outcomes (student retention, faculty satisfaction) might be due in part to differences among higher-level groups or contexts (class size, department size, and so on). Analyses of these data using ordinary linear regression methods are problematic, as the underlying structure of the data often leads to violations of the assumptions of independence intrinsic to these models. Through HLM, we are able to model these dependencies and to examine how differential characteristics in the higher-level contexts help to explain variation in individual or lower-level outcomes. An HLM approach can also be used in place of repeated-measures analysis of variance in longitudinal studies. By viewing a series of repeated observations as lower-level outcomes nested within the individual, researchers are able to explore the effects of higher-level individual characteristics (gender, age) on the patterns of change in the lower-level outcomes over time.

Figure 1.1 represents a prototype situation for nested or clustered cross-sectional data from a single institution. In this figure, potential data of interest such as student persistence, gender, or first-year grade point average (GPA) reside at level one, the lowest level of the hierarchy. These level-one characteristics vary across individuals within the same department as well as between departments. Students are nested within different departments, and these departments may vary in terms of supports in place for mentoring new students or size of faculty in that department. These level-two characteristics vary between departments, but they do not vary between students within the same department. Finally, data representing the institution, such as total endowment or selectivity of undergraduate admissions, are common to all departments and all students within departments at that institution; there is no variability at the institutional level for the prototype model shown. Thus, while there seems to be three levels to the hierarchy, the analysis of outcomes at the student level would be examined through a two-level HLM: students nested within departments. More complex structures are easily accommodated in the HLM environment in both cross-sectional and longitudinal studies. If this cross-sectional data collection scheme were

Figure 1.1. Prototype of Nested or Clustered Data: Students Nested Within Departments

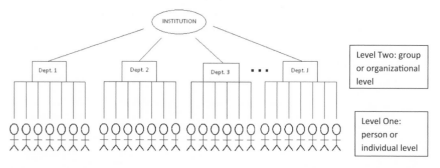

implemented at multiple institutions (see Hox, 1998, and Maas and Hox, 2005, for discussion of factors related to sample sizes at different levels), variability in institutional-level characteristics can be measured and examined, and the influence of institutional context as well as departmental context on student outcomes can be examined through a three-level HLM. If repeated observations of the outcome are collected on all students over a four-year period, such as end-of-year GPA, these repeated measurements reside at the lowest level of data collection; they are nested within students, who are nested within departments, and as a result would add a third level to the analytical design.

Whether the data of interest are longitudinal or cross-sectional, multilevel analyses are concerned with the study of variation. Just as in standard (single-level) regression, the goal of multilevel analysis is to attempt to explain variability, which implies that the outcome of interest can be reliably modeled through a well-chosen or predefined set of predictors, covariates, or explanatory variables. As the multilevel example illustrates, variability exists at each level of a multilevel analysis, and predictors or explanatory variables can exist at different levels as well. Overall, the primary motivation for employing multilevel analysis is to examine and understand the nature of the many different kinds of variability present in the data (Gelman and Hill, 2007). In doing so, we attempt to model the outcomes of interest by examining how group-level or individual-level characteristics are related to lowest-level outcomes.

An assumption in standard regression is that the observations or data subjected to analysis are statistically independent. With nested data, this assumption is clearly violated. Research has consistently shown that for clustered data, observations obtained from persons within the same cluster tend to exhibit more similarity to each other than to observations from different clusters. This similarity leads to underestimation of the standard errors for regression parameter estimates and inflates Type I error even when the similarity is mild (Donner, Birkett, and Buck, 1981; Sudman, 1985; Kenny and Judd, 1986; Murray and Hannon, 1990; Kish, 1995; Fowler, 2001). Cluster homogeneity is commonly measured through the intraclass correlation coefficient (ICC), which can be interpreted as the familiar Pearson correlation between two observations from the same cluster (Donner and Klar, 2000). In a two-level design, the ICC represents the proportion of total variance in the outcome that is captured by differences between the clusters or groups. When no variability is present between the clusters or groups, the value of the ICC is zero, and the assumption of independence among all individuals in the sample is justified. However, in the presence of between-cluster variability, the value of the ICC is positive, indicating a lack of independence, which invalidates standard regression models where clustering is ignored. The presence of ICC supports the adoption of a multilevel approach to analyzing the data, incorporating critical features of the hierarchical structure of the data into the analysis.

Clustered data may arise due to the existence of intact groups within an institution or by design if, for example, first-year students are randomly assigned to small-group mentoring activities to boost student engagement. Another situation in which IR researchers may be presented with clustered data is through sampling convenience. For example, requesting that all students within randomly selected intact courses complete a survey on first-year experiences would yield a more practical and feasible design relative to a sample based on a random selection of students across the entire college or university. However, such clustered samples have limitations as well as strengths that can affect how data may be interpreted. Whether naturally occurring or by intent, the structure of clustered data involves collecting information from clusters or groups of individuals experiencing a common phenomenon or event. In an IR setting, these common phenomena could arise from attending the same class or being in the same degree program. Regardless of the nature of the cluster, the ICC is found through decomposition of total variance in an outcome of interest into its within-group and between-group components; the ICC represents the proportion of variance that is between groups (Raudenbush and Bryk, 2002).

Historical Approaches to Analyzing Data with a Multilevel Structure

Prior to the advent of specialized software devoted to multilevel data, researchers often used two approaches when confronted with clustered or nested data: aggregation and disaggregation. Although multilevel models may eliminate the particular kinds of bias prevalent in these earlier approaches, we review them here to underscore the need for researchers to avoid the kinds of fallacies that earlier methods may have encouraged and to focus instead on methodologically appropriate and ethical practices for multilevel data (American Statistical Association, 1999; Goldstein, 2011).

In an aggregation approach, researchers sometimes averaged the lower-level data within a cluster or group and then used these averages as outcomes or predictor variables in a single-level analysis model. W. S. Robinson's seminal 1950 article on ecological correlations (reprinted in the *International Journal of Epidemiology*, 2009) describes an ecological correlation as the statistical correlation among groups of individuals. It was fairly common at that time to use ecological correlations as if they represented the correlations among the underlying individual-level data; the ecological fallacy refers to the inferential problems inherent in using group-level data to generalize to individual-level relationships. Robinson used 1930 census data to describe correlations among county- or region-level illiteracy rates and the percentage of African Americans in that region. His data showed the ecological correlation to be .946, while the individual-level correlation between illiteracy and race was .203. Since the publication of Robinson's work, researchers have continued to examine and caution against the ecological fallacy, with implications for the importance of context in multilevel studies (for example, Schwartz, 1994; Susser, 1994; Diez-Roux, 1998; Oakes, 2009; Goldstein, 2011).

In a disaggregation approach, researchers disregarded the tendency for data from persons within distinct groups or geographical regions to be correlated and ignored the multilevel structure of the data completely. Thus, all data was analyzed as if it arose at the individual level, and group-relevant variables would retain the same value for all persons within the same group. Such an approach clearly violates the traditional assumption of independence necessary for valid statistical tests. Consequently, standard errors are underestimated and probability values for statistical tests are too small, leading to the potential for overstating statistical significance of the resulting research findings. These issues have been well documented by sampling methodologists and multilevel researchers (for example, Kish, 1995; Murray, 1998; Raudenbush and Bryk, 2002).

Much of the literature on levels-of-analysis problems has focused on the ecological fallacy, but researchers are also cautioned against the atomistic fallacy, which occurs while drawing inferences based on individual-level data and generalizing these inferences to group-level associations (Diez-Roux, 1998). Both kinds of fallacies can be avoided by careful consideration of the level at which data are collected (individual versus group) and by consistent representation of these levels in the statistical model. Hierarchically structured data, such as those that occur with most institutional research data, are uniquely represented through multilevel models.

Importance of Advancements in Statistical Methods in Institutional Research

Pascarella and Terenzini (1991, 2005) are renowned for their emphasis on methodological rigor in understanding how colleges affect students. Their work documents the importance of remaining current in statistical and research methods for those conducting institutional research. In addition to advancing theories and models for student change, theory development and research must be matched by advances in statistical methodologies. For example, two decades ago, Pascarella and Terenzini's 1991 volume discussed, in part, the strengths and limitations of the use of meta-analysis as an approach to aggregating and comparing results across research studies. In their 2005 volume, while still characterizing limitations to meta-analysis in their updated literature for the new edition, they specifically recognize the profound advances in statistical methods that have occurred over the past 20 years or so, including MLM. The capacity for multilevel models to strengthen our understanding of how colleges and universities affect students cannot be overemphasized. In the next section, we highlight some of the ways in which multilevel models may be used in institutional research, before turning to our introduction of model notation and interpretation.

Research Questions in Institutional Research

Colleges and universities are complex organizations involving countless interactions among students, faculty, staff, and administration. These interactions occur among organizational entities made up of departments, schools, and colleges, each with unique policies, practices, and values. Observations of student achievement, faculty productivity, and other important performance indicators may be affected by group-level similarities based on these organizational structures. In addition, increased reliance on institutional data for strategic planning, accreditation, accountability, and performance improvement presents a significant challenge for IR professionals (Brittingham, O'Brien, and Alig, 2008; Voorhees, 2008). Similarly, the increasing demand for comparative analysis across institutions for the purpose of performance benchmarking requires that analytical models be developed that accommodate potential heterogeneity across institutions, states, and regions (Yorke, 2010). To effectively assess institutional performance, IR professionals require analytical tools that facilitate comparative analysis across these heterogeneous groups and permit the evaluation of group effects on individual-level performance. By learning and employing multilevel techniques to provide actionable information based in this broad institutional perspective, IR offices can position themselves as key partners in organizational dialogue and decision making (Parmley, 2009).

As the higher education landscape is transformed by demands for increased accountability, a growing emphasis on global demographics, aging faculty and facilities, an increased dependency on technology, and ongoing shifts in the economic climate, IR offices have become an invaluable part of institutional strategic positioning and planning efforts (Voorhees, 2008). To properly inform and support these activities, IR professionals must provide analyses of a wide variety of performance indicators involving data collected from all areas of the institution. Enrollment management measures including college choice, transition to college, student flow, attrition and retention, and student graduation rates are used to shape policy, inform practice, and guide strategic investment across the institution. Findings from studies involving student-centered indicators such as engagement, satisfaction, safety, and health and wellness are utilized to enhance student development. Analyses of campus-centered variables such as campus climate, diversity, sustainability, and service may be used to transform organizational culture. Institutional researchers may also be involved with efforts to effectively deploy campus human resources through the analysis of workplace satisfaction, faculty and staff work, and organizational training effectiveness. Evaluation of performance in academic affairs incorporates measures of student achievement, assessment, program completion, student placements, faculty activity and productivity, and program effectiveness. As a result of this broad involvement, IR is well positioned to facilitate collaborative decision making, which transcends the multilevel organizational structures typical of college and universities (Leimer, 2009).

Introducing Multilevel Models

Our goal in this chapter is to introduce the IR researcher to the concepts and language of multilevel models. We present a discussion of the ways in which institutional researchers can use and interpret multilevel models, and we identify their strengths as well as limitations through this discussion. There are several different notational frameworks with which to represent multilevel models, and here we utilize the approach of Raudenbush and Bryk (2002), although familiarity with other representations, such as that presented in Snijders and Bosker (1999), is recommended. We focus in this introductory chapter on models where outcomes are continuous and measured at least at the interval level, but the literature on multilevel models for dichotomies, ordinal outcomes, counts, or times-to-event data—as well as longitudinal and latent-growth models—is fairly extensive and builds naturally on applications for continuous outcomes (see, for example, Snijders and Bosker, 1999; Raudenbush and Bryk, 2002; Singer and Willett, 2003; Gelman and Hill, 2007; O'Connell, Goldstein, Rogers, and Peng, 2008).

We begin with a simple example and introduce the development and interpretation of multilevel models by posing a series of questions that can be represented by different models. Suppose a university is interested in increasing its enrollment of underrepresented students (African American, Asian American, Hispanic, and American Indian) into STEM disciplines (science, technology, engineering, and mathematics). As a first step, the university wants to examine how graduating seniors' perceptions of their college experiences vary across academic units based on student race/ethnicity and selected characteristics of their home department or unit, including its type (STEM, non-STEM) and the proportion of underrepresented students in the department. A random sample of graduating students from all departments has been obtained.

In this example, variables are included at two levels. At the student level, we have the scores on senior student experiences, which may be captured through a self-reported rating scale of 1 through 10, with 10 representing more favorable experiences. Thus, the outcome Y_{ij} will represent the experiences rating for the ith senior in the jth department. We also have a student-level predictor, X_{ij}, which is a dummy-coded variable indicating whether the ith senior in the jth department is from an underrepresented group (1 = yes, 0 = no). Two department-level predictors are included, and we use W rather than X to distinguish between variables at level one (Xs) versus level two (Ws). For our example, W_{1j} is dummy-coded to represent whether or not the jth department falls under the identification of a STEM discipline (1 = yes, 0 = no), and our second level-two predictor W_{2j} is the proportion of students from underrepresented groups in the jth department.

On Average, Do Seniors' Experience Ratings Differ Across Departments? In a multilevel analysis, the first model that is typically fit is referred to as the empty model, and it is the same as a one-way analysis of variance (ANOVA) model with random effects (Raudenbush and Bryk, 2002).

$$\text{Level 1:} \quad Y_{ij} = \beta_{0j} + r_{ij}$$

$$\text{Level 2:} \quad \beta_{0j} = \gamma_{00} + u_{0j}$$

As with all statistical analyses, simplifying assumptions are made regarding the data. Although beyond the scope of this discussion, it is strongly recommended that readers investigate the validity of these assumptions through model comparisons and residual diagnostics. Here we assume that the department rating scores follow a normal distribution, with department-specific means, β_{0j}, and a common variance within all departments, σ^2. The existence of this common variance constitutes the homogeneity of variance assumption, which can readily be tested, and relaxed, in existing software for multilevel models. We also assume that the department means themselves vary based on a normal distribution with an overall mean γ_{00} and variance τ_{00}. Finally, we assume there is no correlation between the residuals at level one and those at level two. This set of assumptions can be collectively written as:

$$r_{ij} \sim iid \, N\left(0, \sigma^2\right)$$

$$u_{0j} \sim iid \, N\left(0, \tau_{00}\right)$$

$$Cov\left(r_{ij}, u_{0j}\right) = 0$$

The level-one model tells us about the variability in experience scores that exists within each academic unit; and the level-two model tells us about the variability between the academic units. All else being equal, a larger σ^2 would suggest that, within departments, there is a great deal of individual variability in seniors' experience rating scores. Similarly, all else being equal, a larger τ_{00} would suggest that there is a large amount of variability between departments in average experience rating scores.

By substituting the level-two model into the level-one equation (where the same set of assumptions hold), the two models representing variability at each level of data can be combined into a mixed model:

$$Y_{ij} = \gamma_{00} + u_{0j} + r_{ij}$$

The complex pattern of variation that is the defining characteristic of hierarchically structured data can be seen directly in this mixed-model form. In particular, two sets of residuals are used to represent the variation between and within the academic units, and their relative contribution to total variability is captured by the ICC. As described earlier, the ICC is a measure of the proportion of total variance (between + within) that can be attributed to the group or cluster; it provides an assessment of how strongly the clusters contribute to dependency in the data:

$$ICC = \frac{\tau_{00}}{\tau_{00} + \sigma^2}$$

The value of the ICC will be positive, even when the contextual group effect is very small. Ignoring the existence of a positive ICC, even if close to zero, can have serious consequences for validity of hypothesis tests as well as for understanding and examining patterns of variability in the data.

Due to the complexity of the model and its partitioning of variance into level-specific components, estimation of model parameters requires iterative strategies generally solved through maximum likelihood procedures. In this simplest of models, the single fixed effect is γ_{00}, which represents the single point estimate for the grand mean of all departments' experience rating scores. Simultaneously, estimates are generated for the variance components, which summarize the contribution of random effects to the model at their respective levels (that is, level one: $\sigma^2 = \text{var}(r_{ij})$, and level two: $\tau_{00} = \text{var}(u_{0j})$).

Multilevel research attempts to explain variability in the dependent variable based on the predictors' contributions to their level-specific variation. Thus we use Xs to attempt to reduce individual variation, σ^2, and we use Ws to try to account for between-group variability, τ_{00}. Inferential accuracy of the statistical tests of the fixed effects and the variance components rests on the validity of assumptions placed on the data. Generally, a t-test is used for testing whether a specific fixed effect (that is, γ_{00}) is equal to zero; and a Wald test or a chi-square test is used to assess whether a variance component (for example, τ_{00}) is statistically different from zero (see Chapter 2, this volume, for alternative approaches to significance testing based on deviance comparisons). As variance is explained or accounted for, improved understanding of the phenomena of interest is achieved.

Does the Senior Student's Status as a Member of an Underrepresented Group Affect Ratings of Perceived College Experiences? Once we have established that differences in outcomes between academic units exist, we next consider the effect of a level-one covariate, senior's group membership status. Status is a dichotomous predictor, with 1 indicating that the student is a member of an underrepresented group at the

NEW DIRECTIONS FOR INSTITUTIONAL RESEARCH • DOI: 10.1002/ir

university and 0 indicating otherwise. As a student-level predictor, status is entered at level one:

$$\text{Level 1: } Y_{ij} = \beta_{0j} + \beta_{1j}X_{ij} + r_{ij}$$

$$\text{Level 2: } \beta_{0j} = \gamma_{00} + u_{0j}$$

$$\beta_{1j} = \gamma_{10} + u_{1j}$$

This particular model is referred to as a random coefficients model. Note that an additional residual term is now included at level two. This residual term implies that the effect of status on ratings of college experience is expected to vary across academic units—that is, the slope for the status variable is not constant across departments, but varies between them. Thus, the intercepts and slopes from the level-one model vary at random. Within any given department, the expected average experience rating for non-underrepresented students (that is, when $X_{ij} = 0$) is β_{0j}, and the expected average experience rating for underrepresented students (that is, when $X_{ij} = 1$) is $\beta_{0j} + \beta_{1j}$.

Using back-substitution similar to the empty model, we can derive the mixed-model expression for this random coefficients model:

$$Y_{ij} = \gamma_{00} + \gamma_{10}X_{ij} + u_{0j} + u_{1j}X_{ij} + r_{ij}$$

Averaging across all departments in this example, the mean experience rating is γ_{00} for non-underrepresented students, and the mean experience rating for underrepresented students is $\gamma_{00} + \gamma_{10}$. A significant t-test result for γ_{10} implies that the mean difference in experience ratings between non-underrepresented students and underrepresented students is statistically different from zero. The residual for the slope captures variability in the effect of senior's underrepresentation status across schools. If this effect does not vary between departments, then all of the u_{1j}s would equal zero, and the estimated slope for status would be constant for all departments. Thus, the slope parameter can be fixed, or held constant, rather than be free to vary across groups.

The addition of a single predictor at level one has important implications for the covariance structure of the model:

$$r_{ij} \sim iid\ N\left(0, \sigma^2\right)$$

$$\begin{bmatrix} u_{0j} \\ u_{1j} \end{bmatrix} \sim iid\ N\left[\begin{pmatrix} 0 \\ 0 \end{pmatrix}, \begin{pmatrix} \tau_{00} & \tau_{01} \\ \tau_{10} & \tau_{11} \end{pmatrix}\right]$$

The covariance structure of the level-two residuals is often written as $iid\ N(\underline{0}, \mathbf{T})$ where the size of the symmetric covariance matrix $\mathbf{T}$ depends on the number of randomly varying coefficients at level one. This structure is more complex than in the previous empty model, due to the accommodation of variability in slopes for the level-one covariate. The covariance term, τ_{01}, captures the association between the level-one intercepts and slopes. If we set the slope variance, τ_{11}, to zero, we end up with a simpler model but one in which the effect of a student's underrepresentation status is constant across all departments.

Adding a relevant predictor to the level-one model should account for some of the individual-level variance contributing to σ^2. The reduction in variance achieved over the empty model can be assessed by comparing the two variances:

$$\frac{\sigma^2_{empty\_model} - \sigma^2_{RC\_model}}{\sigma^2_{empty\_model}}$$

This simple proportion can be used to calculate variance accounted for in more complex models as well. If the expression is zero or negative, it suggests that no variance was reduced over the empty model. Negative results may sometimes arise, due to the maximum likelihood estimation procedures used to fit these kinds of models.

Note that we were able to directly interpret the intercepts, β_{0j}, in this random coefficients model. In all regression models, the intercept is interpreted as the prediction when the covariate is zero. For a dummy-coded variable such as underrepresentation status, this process is straightforward, but for many continuous variables—for example, GPA—there may be no interpretable zero. In single-level regression we are rarely bothered by this fact because our attention is focused on the slopes, which represent effects of different predictors on the outcome. In the multilevel framework, it is often optimal to have intercepts that are directly interpretable. A process called centering is usually employed with continuous level-one predictors to provide a more meaningful interpretation to the intercepts.

Centering has several forms in the multilevel framework, and although it yields a meaningful intercept, it can change the degree of variability in the model and thus should be used carefully. Group-mean centering, or centering within contexts (CWC), of a covariate subtracts the mean of each group's covariate score from each participant's original covariate score: $(X_{ij} - \bar{X}_{.j})$. Centering at the grand mean (CGM) of the covariate subtracts the overall mean from each participant's score: $(X_{ij} - \bar{X}_{..})$. Substituting either of these into the level-one random coefficients model has no effect on the estimation for the fixed-effect slopes, but it does change the quantity being estimated, and thus our interpretation, for the intercepts. For example, with CWC the level-one equation becomes $Y_{ij} = \beta_{0j} + \beta_{1j}(X_{ij} - \bar{X}_{.j}) + r_{ij}$. The intercept is now the predicted value of Y_{ij} when X_{ij} is at the group mean, that is, for a participant who is at the average value of the predictor for their group. Similarly for CGM, the intercept becomes the prediction when X_{ij} is at the grand mean for the sample, or for a participant who is at the average value of the covariate for all persons in the sample: $Y_{ij} = \beta_{0j} + \beta_{1j} (X_{ij} - \bar{X}) + r_{ij}$. Centering is used primarily for continuous covariates, but Raudenbush and Bryk (2002) provide a discussion of its use with effect-coded dichotomous variables. Other recommended sources for the use of centering and its implications in multilevel analyses include Hofmann and Gavin (1998), Paccagnella (2006), and Enders and Tofighi (2007).

Can Contextual Variables (Characteristics of Academic Units) Help to Explain Variability in Intercepts and Slopes across Units? In addition to reducing within-unit variance by the inclusion of level-one predictors, the random coefficients model provides us with baseline information about how much variability in the level-one intercepts and slopes exists between the academic departments. In our example, we have two level-two covariates: W_{1j} is a STEM indicator variable for whether the jth department is a STEM discipline (1 = yes, 0 = no), and W_{2j} is the proportion of students from underrepresented groups within the jth department. We include these variables at level two to examine their contribution to predictions of both the slopes and intercepts from level one.

$$\text{Level 1: } Y_{ij} = \beta_{0j} + \beta_{1j}X_{ij} + r_{ij}$$

$$\text{Level 2: } \beta_{0j} = \gamma_{00} + \gamma_{01}W_{1j} + \gamma_{02}W_{2j} + u_{0j}$$

$$\beta_{1j} = \gamma_{10} + \gamma_{11}W_{1j} + \gamma_{12}W_{2j} + u_{1j}$$

Because this model retains the same level-one model as the previous random coefficients model, the structure of the variance and covariance components remains the same, although estimates are likely to differ— and be smaller, if variance has been explained by the inclusion of level-two predictors:

$$r_{ij} \sim iid\ N\left(0, \sigma^2\right)$$

$$\begin{bmatrix} u_{0j} \\ u_{1j} \end{bmatrix} \sim iid\ N\left[\begin{pmatrix} 0 \\ 0 \end{pmatrix}, \begin{pmatrix} \tau_{00} & \tau_{01} \\ \tau_{10} & \tau_{11} \end{pmatrix}\right]$$

Models of this type, which include both level-one and level-two predictors, are often called intercepts and slopes as outcomes models, or conditional models. We can assess reduction in between-group variance in the intercepts and slopes using an approach similar to that taken to find the reduction in within-group variance when we discussed the random coefficients model. In the next expression, q refers to the qth random coefficient (including the intercept) from the level-one model. Thus, our assessment of reduction in variance would allow us to verify if the collection of Ws added into each equation helped to improve predictions of the slopes and intercepts, respectively.

$$\frac{\tau_{qq(base)} - \tau_{qq(full)}}{\tau_{qq(base)}}$$

The conditional model can be used to answer questions regarding how characteristics of academic departments, such as whether they represent a STEM discipline or the proportion of students from underrepresented groups currently enrolled in the department, are related to mean perceived experience ratings for non-underrepresented students in that department, intercept β_{0j}, or to differences in perceived experience ratings between non- and underrepresented students, slope β_{1j}.

Averaging across departments in the conditional model, γ_{00} tells us the expected mean perceived experience score for non-underrepresented students not enrolled in a STEM department ($W_{1j} = 0$) and for departments in which the proportion of students from underrepresented groups is zero ($W_{2j} = 0$). Also in the level-two intercept equation, γ_{01} is the fixed effect for W_{1j} and represents the expected difference in the mean perceived experience ratings of non-underrepresented students for those in STEM disciplines, holding W_{2j} constant. The increase or decrease in mean ratings attributed to proportion of students from underrepresented groups in the department, holding STEM discipline constant, is captured by the effect of W_{2j} (γ_{02}). Statistical tests for these coefficients would indicate whether they are statistically different from zero or not.

The fixed effects in the level-two slope equation can be interpreted in a similar fashion. Averaging across departments, γ_{10} represents the mean effect of being a student from an underrepresented group on the perceived experience ratings, and this effect is conditional on whether the student's academic unit is a STEM department (γ_{11}) and on the unit's proportion of underrepresented students (γ_{12}). Again, significance tests for these coefficients provide information on their statistical contribution to the level-two model being examined.

When level-two predictors have a significant effect on a level-one slope estimate, such as may be expected through γ_{11} and γ_{12}, a cross-level interaction has occurred. A cross-level interaction is an interaction between a level-one predictor X and a level-two predictor W. The mixed-model expression shows this quite clearly:

$$Y_{ij} = \gamma_{00} + \gamma_{01}W_{1j} + \gamma_{02}W_{2j} + \gamma_{10}X_{ij} + \gamma_{11}X_{ij}W_{1j} + \gamma_{12}X_{ij}W_{2j} + u_{0j} + u_{1j}X_{ij} + r_{ij}$$

This model may be simplified by fixing the level-one coefficients that show little or no variability or by removing nonsignificant predictors or

cross-level interactions. Consistent with good statistical modeling practice, decisions to include or exclude variables and interaction terms should
also be based on theory and the purpose of the research, not just on the
results of a statistical test.

We now have much of the basic notation necessary to support the
design and analysis of multilevel models within an IR setting. Other chapters in this book will strengthen these concepts and solidify their application to authentic research practice. Before summarizing, however, we turn
to a few remaining issues to complete this chapter.

Designing Research within Institutional Research Settings

Maximum likelihood is a large-sample estimation method and requires
sufficiently large samples for valid inferences. Unfortunately, no single
magic number indicates when a large enough sample size has been
obtained for a specific research question, and many factors can influence
the optimal sample size necessary to reliably detect effects of interest.
Maas and Hox (2005) discuss the impact that design and sample/popula-
tion features have on the quality of estimation and the resulting inferences
based on a multilevel analysis, including the sizes of variances and covari-
ances and the ICC.

The size of the ICC for a particular outcome variable affects the size
of standard errors of the regression coefficients for predictor variables,
which in turn form the denominator of many statistical tests and contribute to the endpoints of confidence intervals for point estimates of those
regression coefficients. In the sampling literature on cluster and other
complex samples, the impact of the ICC is generally characterized through
the design effect, or "deff," which represents how much the standard
errors from a clustered design are underestimated relative to a simple random sample (SRS): $\text{deff} = 1 + (m - 1) * \text{ICC}$, where m = average cluster or
group size (Kish, 1995; Murray, 1998). A sampling design that mimics an
SRS has a deff of 1.0; clustering increases the design effect, which indicates that the assumption of independence of observations is violated,
making traditional tests of significance biased. The design effect is also
referred to as the inflation factor because it tells us how much the sampling variance is inflated over the sampling variance expected in the gold
standard of an SRS, due to the clustering effect (the ICC). In design planning, estimates of expected ICC are singularly important, because the balance between number of level-one and number of level-two units is
typically weighted toward a larger number of level-two units as ICC
increases, and the power to detect important group differences will dimin-
ish as the level-two sample size decreases, all else being equal (Moerbeek,
van Breukelen, and Berger, 2000; Spybrook, 2008). The relationships
among ICC, sample size at multiple levels, and power are the driving force

behind calls for researchers to publish the ICCs obtained from their research studies (Murray, Varnell, and Blitstein, 2004).

A dilemma in most multilevel research design scenarios arises because recruiting another unit or group is often more difficult—and more costly—than recruiting additional participants from an already sampled unit or group. Institutional researchers often have access to very large samples given the size of their institutions, but a larger level-one sample size will not compensate for the decrease in power for detecting group-specific differences or effects given a small level-two sample size. Thus, studies in IR need to be carefully planned to attain their research goals with sufficient power.

Resources are available for estimating sample sizes based on desired or expected design characteristics. The Optimal Design software (Liu and others, 2006; Spybrook, 2008) is freely accessible on the Internet from the W.T. Grant Foundation (http://www.wtgrantfoundation.org/resources/overview/research_tools) and allows researchers to manipulate features of a design to optimize power under different research or statistical constraints. In addition, the literature and resources for optimizing power given design and cost limitations continue to expand (for example, see Moerbeek, van Breukelen, and Berger, 2000, 2001; Raudenbush and Liu, 2000, 2001; Bloom, 2005; Hedges and Rhoads, 2010). For optimal design of studies in IR, researchers should ensure that their designs are strong enough to match the importance of the research questions being asked in this field (for example, see Moerbeek, van Breukelen, and Berger, 2000, 2001; Raudenbush and Liu, 2000, 2001; Bloom, 2005; Hedges and Rhoads, 2010).

Summary

We conclude with a brief summary of why MLM is important to researchers in IR.

1. If our data are hierarchical, and most IR data are indeed hierarchical, MLM yields valid estimates of variable effects or group differences by directly taking into account the nature of clustering inherent in the data.
2. Ignoring the hierarchical structure of IR data limits the opportunity to examine whether and how differences in patterns of relationships between predictors and outcomes vary across groups, such as academic units, schools, or other definable levels in the data.
3. Study design features can be used to advantage in designing future studies to replicate or qualify observed or expected effects, thus furthering the opportunity to strengthen and build upon research in IR.
4. In multilevel analyses, the ICC can be directly measured and the impact of clustering accounted for in statistical models, thus decreasing tendency for Type I error and flawed conclusions.

5. Contexts do matter, and student's individual and collective college experiences are relevant to many stakeholders (state policy makers, university administrators, professors, parents, and students themselves). IR researchers have an obligation to examine outcomes and enhance this experience for students through ethical and valid methodologies.

References

American Statistical Association. "Ethical Guidelines for Statistical Practice." 1999. Retrieved August 18, 2011, from http://www.amstat.org/about/ethicalguidelines.cfm.

Bloom, H. S. "Randomizing Groups to Evaluate Place-Based Programs." In H. S. Bloom (ed.), *Learning More from Social Experiments: Evolving Analytic Approaches.* New York: Russell Sage, 2005.

Brittingham, B., O'Brien, P. M., and Alig, J. L. "Accreditation and Institutional Research: The Traditional Role and New Dimensions." In D. G. Terkla (ed.), *More Than Just Data.* New Directions for Higher Education, no. 141. San Francisco: Jossey-Bass, 2008.

Diez-Roux, A. V. "Bringing Context Back into Epidemiology: Variables and Fallacies in Multilevel Analysis." *American Journal of Public Health,* 1998, *88*(2), 216–222.

Donner, A., Birkett, N., and Buck, C. "Randomization by Cluster: Sample Size Requirements and Analysis." *American Journal of Epidemiology,* 1981, *114*(6), 906–914.

Donner, A., and Klar, N. *Design and Analysis of Cluster Randomization Trials in Health Research.* London: Arnold, 2000.

Enders, C. K., and Tofighi, D. "Centering Predictor Variables in Cross-Sectional Multilevel Models: A New Look at an Old Issue." *Psychological Methods,* 2007, *12*(2), 121–138.

Fowler, F. J. *Survey Research Methods.* (3rd ed.). Newbury Park, Calif.: Sage Publications, 2001.

Gelman, A., and Hill, J. *Data Analysis Using Regression and Multilevel/Hierarchical Models.* New York: Cambridge University Press, 2007.

Goldstein, H. "Ethical Aspects of Multilevel Modeling." In A.T. Panter and S. K. Sterba (eds.), *Handbook of Ethics in Quantitative Methodology.* New York: Routledge, 2011.

Hedges, L. V., and Rhoads, C. "Statistical Power Analysis in Educational Research (NCSER 2010–3006)." Washington, DC: National Center for Special Education Research, Institute of Education Sciences, U.S. Department of Education, 2010. Retrieved August 18, 2011, from http://ies.ed.gov/ncser/pubs/20103006/pdf/20103006.pdf.

Hofmann, D. A., and Gavin, M. B. "Centering Decisions in Hierarchical Linear Models: Implications for Research in Organizations." *Journal of Management,* 1998, *23*, 723–744.

Hox, J. "Multilevel Modeling: When and Why?" In I. Balderjahn, R. Mather, and M. Schader (eds.), *Classification, Data Analysis, and Data Highways. Proceedings of the 21st Annual Conference of the Gesellschaft fur Klassifikation.* New York: Springer-Verlag, 1998.

Kenny, D. A., and Judd, C. M. "Consequences of Violating the Independence Assumption in Analysis of Variance." *Psychological Bulletin,* 1986, *99*, 422–431.

Kish, L. *Survey Sampling.* New York: Wiley Classics, 1995. (Originally published 1965.)

Leimer, C. "Taking a Broader View: Using Institutional Research's Natural Qualities for Transformation." In C. Leimer (ed.), *Imagining the Future of Institutional Research.* New Directions for Institutional Research, no. 143. San Francisco: Jossey-Bass, 2009.

Liu, X, and others. "Optimal Design for Multilevel and Longitudinal Research," Version 1.77. HLM Software, 2006.

Maas, C.J.M, and Hox, J. J. "Sufficient Sample Sizes for Multilevel Modeling." *Methodology*, 2005, *1*(13), 86–92.

Moerbeek, M., van Breukelen, G.J.P., and Berger, M.P.F. "Design Issues for Experiments in Multilevel Populations." *Journal of Educational and Behavioral Statistics*, 2000, *25*, 271–284.

Moerbeek, M., van Breukelen, G.J.P., and Berger, M.P.F. "Optimal Experimental Designs for Multilevel Models with Covariates." *Communications in Statistics, Theory and Methods*, 2001, *30*, 2683–2697.

Murray, D. M. *Design and Analysis of Group-Randomized Trials*. New York: Oxford University Press, 1998.

Murray, D. M., and Hannon, P. J. "Planning for the Appropriate Analysis in School-Based Drug-Use Prevention Studies." *Journal of Consulting and Clinical Psychology*, 1990, *58*, 458–468.

Murray, D. M., Varnell, S. P., and Blitstein, J. L. "Design and Analysis of Group-Randomized Trials: A Review of Recent Methodological Developments." *Public Health Matters*, 2004, *94*(3), 423–432.

O'Connell, A. A., Goldstein, J., Rogers, J., and Peng, C. J. "Multilevel Logistic Models for Dichotomous and Ordinal Data." In A. A. O'Connell and D. B. McCoach (eds.), *Multilevel Modeling of Educational Data*. Charlotte, N.C.: Information Age, 2008.

Oakes, J. M. "Commentary: Individual, Ecological and Multilevel Fallacies." *International Journal of Epidemiology*, 2009, *38*(2), 361–368.

Paccagnella, G. "Centering or Not Centering in Multilevel Models: The Role of the Group Mean and the Assessment of Group Effects." *Evaluation Review*, 2006, *30*, 66.

Parmley, K. A. "Raising the Institutional Research Profile: Assessing the Context and Expanding the Use of Organizational Frames." In C. Leimer (ed.), *Imagining the Future of Institutional Research*. New Directions for Institutional Research, no. 143. San Francisco: Jossey-Bass, 2009.

Pascarella, E., and Terenzini, P. *How College Affects Students*. San Francisco: Jossey-Bass, 1991.

Pascarella, E., and Terenzini, P. *How College Affects Students, Vol. 2: A Third Decade of Research*. San Francisco: Jossey-Bass, 2005.

Raudenbush, S. W., and Bryk, A. S. *Hierarchical Linear Models: Applications and Data Analysis Methods*. (2nd ed.). Thousand Oaks, Calif.: Sage Publications, 2002.

Raudenbush, S. W., and Liu, X. F. "Statistical Power and Optimal Design for Multisite Randomized Trials." *Psychological Methods*, 2000, *5*(2), 199–213.

Raudenbush, S. W., and Liu, X. F. "Effects of Study Duration, Frequency of Observation, and Sample Size on Power in Studies of Group Differences in Polynomial Change." *Psychological Methods*, 2001, *6*(4), 387–401.

Robinson, W. S. "Ecological Correlations and the Behavior of Individuals." *Journal of Epidemiology*, 2009, *38*(2), 337–341. (Originally published 1950.)

Schwartz, S. "The Fallacy of the Ecological Fallacy: The Potential Misuse of a Concept and the Consequences." *American Journal of Public Health*, 1994, *84*, 819–824.

Singer, J. D., and Willett, J. B. *Applied Longitudinal Data Analysis: Methods for Studying Change and Event Occurrence*. New York: Oxford University Press, 2003.

Snijders, T.A.B., and Bosker, R. J. *Multilevel Analysis: An Introduction to Basic and Advanced Multilevel Modeling*. London: Sage Publications, 1999.

Spybrook, J. "Power and Sample Size for Classroom and School-Level Interventions." In A. O'Connell and B. McCoach (eds.), *Multilevel Analysis of Educational Data*. Greenwich, Conn.: Information Age, 2008.

Sudman, S. "Mail Surveys of Reluctant Professionals." *Evaluation Review*, 1985, *9*(3), 349–359.

Susser, M. "The Logic in Ecological: I. The Logic of Analysis." *American Journal of Public Health,* 1994, *84*(5), 825–829.

Voorhees, R. A. "Institutional Research's Role in Strategic Planning." In D. G. Terkla (ed.), *More Than Just Data.* New Directions for Higher Education, no. 141. San Francisco: Jossey-Bass, 2008.

Yorke, M. "'Supra-Institutional Research': A Cost-Effective Contribution towards Enhancement." *Journal of Higher Education Policy and Management,* 2010, *32*(3), 261–273.

ANN A. O'CONNELL is a professor of quantitative research, evaluation, and measurement at The Ohio State University.

SANDRA J. REED is a doctoral candidate in quantitative research, evaluation, and measurement at The Ohio State University.

2

In this chapter, we introduce topics related to the estimation of multilevel models and the determination of model fit. We introduce techniques for model specification and comparison and provide recommendations for their application.

Introduction to Estimation Issues in Multilevel Modeling

D. Betsy McCoach, Anne C. Black

This chapter is designed to give the reader a conceptual, nontechnical overview of estimation and model fit issues in multilevel modeling (MLM). The process of MLM generally involves fitting a series of multilevel models that increase in complexity. When conducting multilevel analyses, it is important to balance the need for complexity and the need for parsimony. Therefore, having a solid understanding of issues related to model fit is essential in MLM. To really understand model fit, it is necessary to have at least a conceptual understanding of estimation issues. This chapter deliberately stays at a conceptual level and is not meant to be a thorough mathematical or algorithmic treatment of estimation issues in MLM. It is our hope, however, that this chapter can provide the novice multilevel modeler with an appreciation for the estimation process and a procedure for determining model fit. For a more technical discussion of these issues, the reader should consult Raudenbush and Bryk (2002), where all of these concepts are discussed in greater depth.

Conceptual Introduction to Maximum

Let us begin our overview of estimation by discussing the rationale for and the use of maximum likelihood estimation in MLM. Maximum likelihood estimation techniques provide estimates for the values of the population

NEW DIRECTIONS FOR INSTITUTIONAL RESEARCH, no. 154, Summer 2012 © Wiley Periodicals, Inc.
Published online in Wiley Online Library (wileyonlinelibrary.com) • DOI: 10.1002/ir.20012

parameters that maximize the probability of obtaining the observed data (Singer and Willett, 2003). A likelihood function "describes the probability of observing the sample data as a function of the model's unknown parameters" (p. 66).

When we talk about the probability of observing events, we are implicitly assuming some kind of model. Given the parameters of the model, we can make statements about the probability of observing some event. For example, take the case of a coin toss. We talk about the probability of tossing a head as being .5. More formally, in such a model, we have one parameter, p, the probability of tossing a head, and that parameter p is equal to .5. In probability theory, we know the value of the parameter, and we try to predict future outcomes based on that known parameter. The likelihood, however, turns probability on its head. With likelihood, we already have the data, and we try to determine the most likely value for a parameter, given the data. The goal of maximum likelihood estimation is to find the set of parameter values that makes the actual data most likely to have been observed. For example, if we flip 100 coins and 52 times we flip heads and 48 times we flip tails, we could take the data that we have gathered and ask: What is the most likely parameter value for p, the probability that I will flip a head, given the data that I have collected? The answer in this case would be .52 (see http://statgen.iop.kcl .ac.uk/bgim/mle/sslike_2.html). For a much more detailed and nuanced discussion of likelihood estimation, see Myung (2003).

Reliability in MLM

MLM programs use empirical Bayes estimation to derive the randomly varying level-one coefficients (β_{qj}) (Raudenbush and Bryk, 2002). For simplicity, consider the estimation of the randomly varying intercept, β_{0j}, the "true cluster mean" under the simplest model, the random-effects ANOVA model. Remember, $\beta_{0j} = \gamma_{00} + u_{0j}$. Imagine that you wanted to estimate the "true" mean for cluster j. You could use the sample mean, $\overline{Y}_{.j}$, as an estimate of the true mean. However, the fewer people in the sample, the less confident you would be in your use of $\overline{Y}_{.j}$ as an estimate of the true mean. In the most extreme situation, if you did not have anyone from the cluster j to estimate the true cluster mean, what would your best guess about the mean of cluster j be? It would be the overall mean, γ_{00}. So, when trying to imagine the true mean for a cluster, there are two potential competing estimates: the overall mean across the entire sample, which allows you to "borrow" information from other clusters to estimate the mean of cluster j and the sample mean of cluster j, which is measured with some degree of imprecision. As the sample size in cluster j increases, the precision with which we can estimate the true mean from the sample mean increases; there is less error in our measurement of the true cluster mean based on the sample mean. Empirical Bayes estimation takes these two ways to derive the true school mean and combines them based on the reliability of cluster j. The greater the reliability of the cluster j estimate, the more weight is placed on the sample mean as the estimate of the true school mean. The lower the reliability of the cluster j estimate, the more weight that is placed on γ_{00} as an estimate of the true school mean. Let us return to our two potential estimates of the true school mean, γ_{00} and $\bar{Y}_j$. When would γ_{00} be an especially good estimate of the mean of cluster j? The answer is when there is very little or no between-school variance. When would $\bar{Y}_j$ be an especially poor estimate of the true school mean (especially with small sample sizes)? The answer is when there is a great deal of within-school variance. The reliability of school j incorporates these three pieces of information: the within-school variance σ^2, the between-school variance, τ_{00}, and the number of units per cluster, n_j, into the next formula (Raudenbush and Bryk, 2002):

Reliability of

$$\hat{\beta}_{0j} = \frac{\tau_{00}}{\tau_{00} + \dfrac{\sigma^2}{n_j}}$$

Each cluster has its own estimate of reliability. Holding between- and within-school variance constant, larger cluster sizes (n_j) result in higher reliability. Variance estimates τ_{00} and σ^2 remain constant across schools. Therefore, clusters with larger numbers of units will have larger reliability estimates. However, it is important to remember that larger between-school variance (relative to within-school variance) also increases reliability. Therefore, the reliability will be higher when the group means, β_{0j}, vary substantially across level-two units (holding constant the sample size per group). So increasing group size, increasing homogeneity within clusters, and increasing heterogeneity between clusters all increase reliability. You may recognize the below formula as the formula for intraclass correlation (ICC):

$$\frac{\tau_{00}}{\tau_{00} + \sigma^2}$$

A bit of algebra allows for the reexpression of the reliability formula in terms of ICCs (Raudenbush and Bryk, 2002). Thus, larger ICCs result in higher reliability. This makes conceptual sense given that the ICC represents the ratio of between-school variance to overall variability. Therefore, larger ICCs are indicative of small within-cluster variability, large between-cluster variability, or some combination of the two. Reliability can range from 0 to 1, and the lower bound for the reliability in any given sample is the ICC.

Empirical Bayes Estimation

The empirical Bayes estimate of the true school mean weights the two potential estimates for each cluster according to the reliability for that cluster. The formula for weighting each component of the mean estimate is $\beta_{0j}^* = \lambda_j \bar{Y}_{.j} + (1 - \lambda_j) \hat{\gamma}_{00}$, where λ_j is the reliability of the least squares estimator, $\bar{Y}_{.j}$ for the parameter β_{0j} (Raudenbush and Bryk, 2002). Thus, the higher the reliability of the estimate for cluster j, the more weight is placed on $\bar{Y}_{.j}$ as the estimate of the true cluster mean, β_{0j}. In contrast, the lower the reliability of cluster j estimate, the more weight is placed on $\hat{\gamma}_{00}$ as the estimate of the true cluster mean. If the reliability were 1, the sample mean would be used as an estimate of the true cluster mean. If the reliability were 0, $\hat{\gamma}_{00}$ would be used as the estimate of the true cluster mean. Sometimes the empirical Bayes estimators are referred to as shrinkage estimators. This is because the $\bar{Y}_{.j}$ estimate is "shrunken" toward the model-based estimate, and the empirical Bayes residuals are like ordinary least squares (OLS) estimates of the residuals that are "shrunken" toward zero (Raudenbush and Bryk, 2002).

Deviance

Maximum likelihood estimation techniques provide estimates for the values of the population parameters that maximize the probability of obtaining the observed data (Singer and Willett, 2003). A likelihood function "describes the probability of observing the sample data as a function of the model's unknown parameters" (Singer and Willett, 2003, p. 66). The parameter estimates are those estimates that maximize the likelihood function. When we use maximum likelihood to estimate the parameters of the model, the estimation also provides the likelihood, which easily can be transformed into a deviance statistic (Snijders and Bosker, 1999).

The deviance compares the log-likelihood of the specified model to the log-likelihood of a saturated model that fits the sample data perfectly (Singer and Willett, 2003). Specifically, deviance = –2 (log-likelihood of the current model minus the log-likelihood of the saturated model; –2LL; Singer and Willett, 2003). Therefore, deviance is a measure of the badness of fit of a given model; it describes how much worse the specified model is than the best possible model (Singer and Willett, 2003). Deviance statistics cannot be interpreted directly because deviance is a function of sample size as well as the fit of the model. However, differences in deviance can be interpreted for competing models, if those models are hierarchically nested, use the same data set, and use full maximum likelihood estimation techniques to estimate the parameters. Deviance difference tests are described in detail later in this chapter under "Chi-Square Difference Test."

In full information maximum-likelihood (FIML) estimation, the estimates of the variance and covariance components are conditional upon the point estimates of the fixed effects (Raudenbush and Bryk, 2002). The number of model parameters includes both the fixed effects and the variance and covariance components. Restricted maximum likelihood (REML) estimates of variance-covariance components adjust for the uncertainty about the fixed effects; FIML estimates do not (Raudenbush and Bryk, 2002). When the number of level-two units is large, REML and FIML results will produce similar estimates of the variance components. However, when there are few level-two units, the maximum likelihood estimates of the variance components (τ_{qq}) will be smaller than those produced by REML, and the REML results may be more realistic (Raudenbush and Bryk, 2002). An approximation of the degree of under-estimation of the FIML estimates can be obtained using the formula $(J-F)/J$, where J is the number of clusters and F is the number of fixed effects in the model (Raudenbush and Bryk, 2002). For example, when estimating a model with three fixed effects using a sample containing observations from 20 clusters, the level-two variance components are .85 ($(20-3)/20$) as large in FIML as they are in REML; this represents a sub-stantial underestimate of the variance components when using FIML. However, there is an advantage to using FIML. The deviances of any two nested models that differ in terms of their fixed or random effects can be compared when using FIML. When using REML, the chi-square difference test can be applied only to nested models that differ in their random effects (Snijders and Bosker, 1999).

Standard Error Estimation

One of the key differences between multilevel analyses and more tradi-tional regression or ANOVA based analyses is the estimate of the standard errors (SE) for the fixed effects. Generally speaking, standard errors that fail to take clustering into account will be underestimated, resulting in a higher than nominal Type I error rate. In this section, we briefly describe the estimation of the standard errors for both the fixed effects and the ran-dom coefficients.

Fixed Effects. As we know from more basic analyses, the size of the standard error of an estimate is an indication of how precisely the estimate represents the parameter. The precision of a parameter estimate is inversely related to its variance, or squared standard error. The smaller the variance around the estimate, the greater the precision. Precision is driven by sample size. In the most basic multilevel model (the random effects ANOVA model), the fixed effect of interest is γ_{00}, the grand mean. Because its estimate $\hat{\gamma}_{00}$ is derived from the cluster means, $\overline{Y}_{.j}$, the precision of each $\overline{Y}_{.j}$ determines the precision of $\hat{\gamma}_{00}$. The inverse of the precision of $\hat{\gamma}_{00}$ is its variance, and the square root of the variance is the estimate's standard error. We can express a 95 percent confidence interval (CI) around the estimate as:

$$\hat{\gamma}_{00} \pm 1.96 \sqrt{\frac{1}{\sum \frac{1}{\Delta_j}}}$$

$$\sum \frac{1}{\Delta_j} = \text{sum of the precisions of each } \bar{Y}_j$$

$$\frac{1}{\sum \dfrac{1}{\Delta_j}} \quad \text{(the inverse of the sum of precisions)} = \text{variance (Raudenbush and Bryk, 2002)}$$

In more complex multilevel models in which level-two predictors W_j are added to the level-two model, the variances and SE of their coefficients γ_{qs} also are estimated from the precision of $\bar{Y}_j$ as well as the variances of the W_j (see Raudenbush and Bryk, 2002). The 95 percent CI for a given fixed effect estimate, $\hat{\gamma}_{qs}$, is expressed $\hat{\gamma}_{qs} \pm 1.96$ ($SE \ \gamma_{qa}$).

Level-One Random Coefficients. The standard error for a level-one random coefficient, β_q, assuming normally distributed random effects at level two, is estimated as the square root of the parameter variance, $\sqrt{\tau_{qq}}$ where τ_{qq} is the variance of the β_{qj} parameter around the grand mean γ_{q0}. One can express the 95 percent "plausible range" for values of β_q as $\gamma_{q0} \pm 1.96\sqrt{\tau_{qq}}$.

Hypothesis Testing

Hypothesis testing is one of the most commonly utilized model selection methods (Weakliem, 2004). In MLM, researchers often use chi-square difference tests to compare the fit of two different models. In addition, hypothesis tests are used to evaluate whether fixed effects, random level-one coefficients, and variance components are statistically different from zero (Raudenbush and Bryk, 2002). Finally, general linear hypothesis testing allows researchers to test composite hypotheses about sets of fixed effects (Singer and Willett, 2003).

Fixed effects are tested in the HLM program with a t-test with $df = J - S_q - 1$ (where $S_q = $ the number of Ws for that effect).

For the intercept, the null and alternative hypotheses are represented as:

$$H_0 : \gamma_{00} = 0$$

$$H_1 : \gamma_{00} \neq 0$$

For the slopes:

$$H_0 : \gamma_{qs} = 0$$

$$H_1 : \gamma_{qs} \neq 0$$

The researcher evaluates the probability, p, of observing the given effect under the null hypothesis assumption and makes a decision about rejecting the null hypothesis in favor of the alternative when the probability of observing that effect under the null hypothesis is smaller than some value, usually .05.

Multiparameter tests allow the researcher to evaluate whether two or more parameters are equal. For example, one could test whether a set of effects is equal to zero. Such a test would be useful in evaluating the hypothesis that a level-two variable, such as student gender, has no effect on either the intercept or slope coefficient of an outcome variable, such as mathematical reasoning.

The composite hypothesis is H_0: $\gamma_{0s} = 0$ and $\gamma_{1s} = 0$.

The appropriate test statistic for these contrasts is χ^2 with df equal to the number of simultaneous hypotheses being tested. Thus, if two parameters are being simultaneously tested, the df equals 2. Testing multiple parameters simultaneously can help protect against inflated Type I error rate.

Random effects (variance components) are tested with a chi-square test ($df = J - S_q - 1$, where S_q = the number of Ws for that effect).

For the intercept variance, the null and alternative hypotheses are represented as:

$$H_0: \tau_{00} = 0$$

$$H_1: \tau_{00} > 0$$

For the slope variances, they are:

$$H_0: \tau_{qq} = 0$$

$$H_1: \tau_{qq} > 0$$

The tests of the variance components are one-tailed tests because variances can never be negative. Therefore, we test whether the variance is equal to 0 or greater than 0. These hypotheses evaluate whether there is random between-cluster variation in the intercept, β_{0j}, or the slopes, β_{qj}, around a fixed effect. Statistically significant results indicate that there is variability in β_{qj} across level-two units. A nonstatistically significant chi-square test may indicate the random effect can be fixed to zero. In addition, chi-square difference tests can be used to compare two models that differ in terms of their random effects to determine whether including that random effect improves model fit.

Chi-Square Difference Test. Two models are nested when one model is a subset of the other (Kline, 2005). In other words, in nested models, "the more complex model includes all of the parameters of the simpler model plus one or more additional parameters" (Raudenbush, Bryk, Cheong, and Congdon, 2004, pp. 80–81). If two models are nested, the deviance statistics of two models can be compared directly.

The deviance of the simpler model (D_1) minus the deviance of the more complex model (D_2) provides the change in deviance $(D = \Delta D_1 - D_2)$. The simpler model always will have at least as high a deviance as the more complex model, and generally the deviance of the more complex model will be lower than that of the simpler model. In large samples, the difference between the deviances of two hierarchically nested models is distributed as an approximate chi-square distribution with degrees of freedom equal to the difference in the number of parameters being estimated between the two models (de Leeuw, 2004). We refer to the number of parameters in the larger (less parsimonious) model as p_2 and the number of estimated parameters in the smaller (more parsimonious) model as p_1.

In evaluating model fit using the chi-square difference test, the more parsimonious model (p_1) is preferred, as long as it does not result in significantly worse fit. In other words, if the model with the larger number of parameters fails to reduce the deviance by a substantial amount, the more parsimonious model is retained. Therefore, when the change in deviance (ΔD) exceeds the critical value of chi-square with $(p_2 - p_1)$ degrees of freedom, the difference in the deviances is statistically significant. In this situation, we favor the more complex model. However, if the more complex model does not result in a statistically significant reduction in the deviance statistic, we favor the more parsimonious model.

FIML maximizes the likelihood of the sample data, whereas REML maximizes the likelihood of the residuals (Singer and Willett, 2003). In FIML, the number of reported parameters includes the fixed effects (γ) as well as the variance-covariance components. When using REML, the number of reported parameters includes only the variance and covariance components. To compare two nested models that differ in their fixed effects, it is necessary to use FIML estimation, not REML estimation. REML allows for comparison only of models that differ in terms of their random effects but have the same fixed effects. Because most programs use REML as the default method of estimation, it is important to remember to select FIML estimation to use the change in deviance to compare two hierarchically nested models with different fixed effects.

Consider this model:

$$Y_{ij} = \beta_{0j} + \beta_{1j}(SAT)_{ij} + r_{ij}$$
$$\beta_{0j} = \gamma_{00} + \gamma_{01}(Selectivity)_j + u_{0j}$$
$$\beta_{1j} = \gamma_{10} + \gamma_{11}(Selectivity)_j + u_{1j} \tag{1}$$

Remember, the number of estimated parameters in FIML is equal to the number of fixed effects (γ) plus the number of variance covariance components. In this example, there are four fixed effects (γ_{00}, γ_{01}, γ_{10}, and γ_{11}). In addition, there are four variance covariance components (σ^2, the variance of r_{ij}; τ_{00}, the variance of u_{0j}; τ_{11}, the variance of u_{1j}; and τ_{01}, the covariance of u_{0j} and u_{1j}.). Therefore, there are eight estimated parameters in FIML. In contrast, the number of estimated parameters in REML is simply the number of variance-covariance components (σ^2, the variance of r_{ij}; τ_{00}, the variance of u_{0j}; τ_{11}, the variance of u_{1j}; and τ_{01}, the covariance of u_{0j} and u_{1j}.). In this example, there are four estimated parameters in REML.

Imagine we wanted to compare this model to the next model, a model in which the SAT slope is a function only of school selectivity, and did not contain a random effect.

$$Y_{ij} = \beta_{0j} + \beta_{1j}(SAT)_{ij} + r_{ij}$$
$$\beta_{0j} = \gamma_{00} + \gamma_{01}(Selectivity)_j + u_{0j}$$
$$\beta_{1j} = \gamma_{10} + \gamma_{11}(Selectivity)_j \tag{2}$$

We are no longer estimating a variance for u_{1j} or the covariance of u_{1j} and u_{0j}. Therefore, model 2 contains six estimated parameters in FIML and two estimated parameters in REML. The difference between the deviance of model 1 and model 2 could be compared using either REML or FIML because the two models vary only in their variance-covariance components. Assume that the deviance of model 1 is 32, and the deviance of model 2 is 40; therefore, the difference between the deviances is 8. We compare this to the critical value of χ^2 with two degrees of freedom (which is 5.99). Because 8 is larger than 5.99, we reject the null hypothesis that the simpler model provides an equally good fit to the data. We determine that the fit of the simpler model is statistically significantly worse than that of the more complex model. (Another way of stating this is that the more complex model fits significantly better than the simpler model.) Therefore, we conclude that we cannot make the proposed simplifications, and we opt in favor of the more complex model.

Finally, consider model 3, as compared to our initial model, model 1.

$$Y_{ij} = \beta_{0j} + \beta_{1j}(SAT)_{ij} + r_{ij}$$
$$\beta_{0j} = \gamma_{00} + \gamma_{01}(Selectivity)_j + u_{0j}$$
$$\beta_{1j} = \gamma_{10} + u_{1j} \tag{3}$$

Model 1 includes the cross-level interaction between school selectivity and SAT; model 3 does not. Model 3 contains seven estimated parameters in FIML (three fixed effects: γ_{00}, γ_{01}, and γ_{10}; and four random effects: σ^2, τ_{00}, τ_{11}, and τ_{01}). However, model 3 has four estimated parameters in REML, just as model 1 did. This demonstrates that models 1 and 3 are nested models in FIML but not in REML. Thus, to compare these two models, we must fit the two competing models in FIML to compare the resulting deviances.

NEW DIRECTIONS FOR INSTITUTIONAL RESEARCH • DOI: 10.1002/ir

The largest drawback of the hypothesis testing approach is that it only permits the comparison of nested models. It is often impossible to compare competing hypotheses using nested statistical models (Raftery, 1995). This is especially true when the models embody dissimilar or contradictory views of the process or phenomenon under examination (Raftery, 1995). Because hypothesis testing procedures allow for comparison only of nested models, if we wish to compare two models with different sets of predictors, we cannot use the chi-square difference test or any other hypothesis testing procedure. In this situation, model selection indices, such as the Akaike Information Criterion (AIC) and the Bayesian Information Criterion (BIC), or their variants (such as the sample size adjusted BIC), are particularly helpful because they allow us to rank or compare models with different sets of parameters.

AIC and BIC. Model index comparison approaches, such as AIC and BIC, have received relatively less attention within the educational literature, but their use is quite common within the sociological literature. (See, for example, Weakliem, 2004, *Sociological Methods and Research*, a special issue devoted to model selection issues in sociology.) Information theoretic model selection represents, in some sense, the converse of classical hypothesis testing procedures (Bozdogan, 1987). Information theoretic techniques focus on "choosing a critical value which then determines, approximately, what the significance level is or might be" (Bozdogan, 1987, p. 363); whereas, in statistical significance testing, the researcher sets the probability of Type I error (alpha), which then determines the critical value.

There are several advantages to using the AIC or the BIC rather than relying on deviance statistics and chi-square difference tests to evaluate the goodness of fit of a multilevel model. First, the AIC and BIC allow the comparison of nonnested models. As long as the sample remains constant, AIC and BIC allow the comparison of competing models, whether they are hierarchically nested or not. Second, selection indices such as the AIC and the BIC quantify the degree to which the given model represents an improvement over comparison models.

We believe that the combined use of the AIC and the BIC (in conjunction with chi-square difference tests for nested models) can be quite informative. Although our explanations of the AIC and BIC are conceptually and mathematically simplistic, we believe that they will serve the applied researcher. Those interested in the conceptual and methodological underpinnings of the AIC and the BIC should refer to Schwarz (1978), Bozdogan (1987), Raftery (1995), Zucchini (2000), Burnham and Anderson (2004), and Wagenmakers and Farrell (2004).

Not all software programs provide AIC and BIC measures in their output. HLM does not provide estimates of AIC and BIC; however, SPSS, SAS, R, and Mplus do provide these indices. Both the AIC and the BIC can be computed easily from the deviance statistic. Because AIC and BIC are computed from the deviance statistic, FIML generally is considered the most appropriate estimation method to use when computing information criteria (Verbeke and Molenberghs, 2000).

Akaike Information Criterion. The formula for the AIC is:

$$AIC = D + 2p, \tag{4}$$

where D is deviance and p is the number of parameters estimated in the model.

To compute the AIC, simply multiply the number of parameters by 2 and add this product to the deviance statistic. As you will recall, the deviance (or -2log-likelihood [$-2LL$]) represents the degree "of inaccuracy, badness of fit, or bias when the maximum likelihood estimators of the parameters of a model are used" (Bozdogan, 1987, p. 356). The second term, $2p$, imposes a penalty based on the complexity of the model. When there are several competing models, the model with the lowest AIC value is considered to be the best one. Because the AICs penalty term is equal to $2p$, the deviance must decrease by more than 2 per additional parameter to favor the model with greater numbers of parameters.

Compare this to the chi-square difference test for model selection. The critical value of χ^2 with 1 degree of freedom at $\alpha = .05$ is 3.84. Therefore, when comparing two models that differ by 1 degree of freedom, the chi-square difference test actually imposes a more stringent criterion for rejecting the simpler model. In fact, this is true for comparisons of models that differ by seven or fewer parameters. Using the chi-square difference test will result in an equivalent or more parsimonious model than using the AIC when comparing models that differ by seven or fewer parameters. However, when comparing models that differ by more than seven parameters, the AIC will favor more parsimonious models than the chi-square difference test does.

Bayesian Information Criterion. The BIC is equal to the sum of the deviance and the product of the natural log of the sample size and the number of parameters. The formula for the BIC is:

$$BIC = D + \ln(n) * p, \tag{5}$$

where D is deviance ($-2LL$), p is the number of parameters estimated in the model, and n is the sample size.

Therefore, the BIC imposes a penalty on the number of parameters that is affected directly by the sample size. In multilevel models, it is not entirely clear which sample size should be used with the BIC: the number of units at the lowest level, the number of units at the highest level, or some weighted average of the two. SAS PROC MIXED uses the number of independent sampling units as the sample size when computing the BIC. In contrast, SPSS and R use the level-one sample size in their computation of the BIC. Therefore, even though SPSS and SAS will produce identical −2LL and AIC values, the BIC value will differ across these programs. Because the BIC imposes a steeper per-parameter penalty as the sample size increases, the BIC value produced by SPSS and R will be larger than the BIC value produced by SAS, and it will tend to favor more parsimonious models. Mplus also uses the level-one sample size in the computation of BIC. However, because growth models in Mplus typically would be formulated in the wide or multivariate format, the effective sample size used for the computation of the BIC in Mplus is the number of people in the sample. Thus, the choice of sample size for the computation of the BIC is not without controversy. Future research should address the impact of this choice on model selection. In the meantime, researchers should carefully consider which sample size they are implicitly or explicitly using in their computation of the BIC.

However, even at small sample sizes, the BIC will favor more parsimonious models than the AIC or traditional chi-square difference tests. Given a sample size as low as 50, the penalty for the BIC is 3.912 times the number of parameters. In contrast, the penalty for the AIC is two times the number of parameters, and the rejection region for traditional chi-square difference tests is 3.84 for one parameter, 5.99 for two parameters, and so on.

The model with the lowest BIC is considered to be the best-fitting model. Raftery (1995) provided guidelines for interpreting changes in BIC: subtract the BIC for model 1 from the BIC for model 2 to compute a BIC difference ($BIC_1 - BIC_2$). Raftery suggested that BIC differences ranging from 0 to 2 provide weak evidence favoring model 2 over model 1; BIC differences ranging from 2 to 6 provide positive evidence for favoring model 2; BIC differences ranging from 6 to 10 provide strong evidence favoring model 2; and BIC differences above 10 provide very strong evidence favoring model 2 over model 1.

Proportion Reduction in Variance. In single-level regression models, an important determinant of the utility of the model is the proportion of variance explained by the model, or R^2. Unfortunately, there is no exact multilevel analog to the proportion of variance explained. Variance components exist at each level of the multilevel model; therefore, variance can be accounted for at each level of the model. In addition, in random coefficients models, the relation between an independent variable at level one and the dependent variable can vary as a function of the level-two unit or cluster. Consequently, no constant proportion of variance in the dependent variable is explained by the independent variable. Instead, the variance in the dependent variable that is explained by the independent variable varies by cluster. Finally, because the variance components are estimated using MLM estimation, the estimation of the variance can differ slightly from model to model. Therefore, it is impossible to compute an R^2 value for the entire model. However, both Raudenbush and Bryk (2002) and Snijders and Bosker (1999) have proposed multilevel analogs to R^2. In both cases, the authors provided two separate formulas: one to explain variance at level one and another to explain variance at level two.

Perhaps the most common statistic used to estimate the variance explained is the proportional reduction in variance statistic (Raudenbush and Bryk, 2002). The proportional reduction in variance can be estimated for any variance component in the model. This statistic compares the variance in the more parameterized model to the variance in a simpler baseline model. To compute the proportional reduction in variance, subtract the remaining variance within the more parameterized model from the variance within a baseline model. Then divide this difference by the variance within the baseline model. That statistic is computed:

$$\frac{\hat{\sigma}_b^2 - \hat{\sigma}_f^2}{\hat{\sigma}_b^2} \tag{6}$$

$\hat{\sigma}_b^2 =$ estimated level-one variance for the baseline model
$\hat{\sigma}_f^2 =$ estimated level-one variance for the fitted model (Raudenbush and Bryk, 2002).

At level two, population variance components estimates are represented by $\hat{\tau}_{qq}$ and are given for the intercepts (β_{0j}) and each slope estimate ($\beta_{1j}, \beta_{2j}, \ldots, \beta_{qj}$) that is allowed to randomly vary across clusters. The proportional reduction in the variance of a given slope, β_{qj}, is:

$$\frac{\hat{\tau}_{qqb} - \hat{\tau}_{qqf}}{\hat{\tau}_{qqb}}, \tag{7}$$

where $\hat{\tau}_{qqb}$ is the estimated variance of slope q in the base model and $\hat{\tau}_{qqf}$ is the estimated variance of slope q in the fitted model (Raudenbush and Bryk, 2002).

It should be noted, however, that the proportion reduction in variance statistic does not behave like the familiar R^2. First, the proportion reduction in variance statistic proposed by Raudenbush and Bryk (2002) represents a comparison of one model to another model, and as such it cannot be interpreted as an explanation of the absolute amount of variance in the dependent variable. In addition, the proportion reduction in variance statistic can be negative. This actually happens with some regularity when comparing the level-two intercept variance of a completely null model (a random effects ANOVA model that includes no predictors at level one or level two) to the level-two intercept variance of a model that includes a group mean centered predictor at level one.

Many other methods exist to compute an R^2-type measure for multilevel models. Snijders and Bosker (1994, 1999) have proposed a multilevel

R^2-type statistic that produces measures of proportional reduction in prediction error for level one (the prediction of Y_{ij}) and level two (the prediction of $\bar{Y}_j$). However, these statistics are available only for models that include random intercepts; they are not available for random coefficients models, which include randomly varying slopes. Gelman and Pardoe (2006) also have proposed a measure of explained variance for each level of a multilevel model, and their measure does not require fitting multiple nested models (Roberts, Monaco, Stovall, and Foster, 2011). Roberts and colleagues also suggest heuristics for calculating R^2-like measures within a multilevel framework.

The various multilevel R^2-type statistics just described provide heuristics to compare models in terms of their ability to explain variance. However, these estimates do not provide unequivocal estimates of the variance explained by a model. Multilevel R^2 analogs do help researchers to compare predictive ability of various multilevel models. Therefore, they should be reported within the results section of a multilevel paper. When reporting their R^2 results, researchers should be sure to specify whose method was used to compute the R^2-type measure as well as what the formula that they have used is actually measuring.

Considerations When Choosing and Coding Variables for MLM

MLM is an extension of multiple linear regression to incorporate a more complex residual structure, which allows us to partition variance across the levels of our model. As an extension of multiple regression, the coding schemes for categorical variables employed in multilevel analyses are the same as those used in multiple regression. Thus, researchers should use dummy coding, weighted or unweighted effects coding, or contrast coding for all categorical variables (see Cohen, Cohen, West, and Aiken, 2003, for an excellent discussion of coding for multiple regression analyses). The decision about which coding scheme to use is less important than the description of the coding scheme used and the correct interpretations of the parameter estimates that result from such a coding scheme. Finally, researchers need to create all same-level interactions among categorical or continuous variables in the same manner as they would if they were conducting a multiple regression analysis. Again, the interpretation of the interaction parameter estimates depends on the coding schemes used for the lower-order variables. See Aiken and West (1991) for an excellent discussion of creating and interpreting same-level interactions within a multiple regression framework.

Centering. Continuous level-one variables are usually centered to aid in the interpretability of the intercept and other parameter estimates. For organizational models, the two main centering techniques for lower-level independent variables are grand mean centering and group mean centering. In grand mean centering, the overall mean of the variable is subtracted from all scores. Therefore, the new score captures a person's standing relative to the full sample. In group mean centering, the cluster mean is subtracted from the score for each person in that cluster. As such, the transformed score captures a person's standing relative to his or her cluster. Centering decisions are especially important for the lower-level continuous independent variables because the choice of centering at the lower level(s) affects the interpretation of both the lower- and higher-level parameter estimates. Grand mean centering is a simple transformation of the raw score, but group mean centering is not. There is some debate within the multilevel literature about whether it is preferable to use grand mean centering or group mean centering. However, most experts in hierarchical linear modeling seem to agree on three issues related to centering:

1. The decision to use grand mean or group mean centering should be based on substantive reasons, not just statistical ones. For instance, if the primary research question involves understanding the impact of a level-two variable on the dependent variable and the level variables serve as control variables, grand mean centering may be the most appropriate choice. When level-one variables are of primary research interest, however, group mean centering may be more appropriate. This is because group mean centering removes between-cluster variation from the level-one covariate and provides an estimate of the pooled within-cluster variance (Enders and Tofighi, 2007).
2. When using group mean centering, it is important to introduce an aggregate of the group mean centered variable (or a higher-level variable that measures the same construct) into the analysis. Without an aggregate or contextual variable at level two, all of the information about the between-cluster variability is lost.
3. It is important to explain the centering decision and to interpret the parameter estimates accordingly. Enders and Tofighi (2007) provided an excellent discussion of centering in organizational multilevel models.

In growth models, the time or age variable needs to be centered so that the intercept represents an interpretable value. For linear growth models, the most common technique is to center time at initial status or age at the beginning of the study so that the intercept represents an individual's starting value. In reality, though, the time variable can be centered at any point in the data collection period. Again, the choice of centering in longitudinal models should be substantively driven (Biesanz and others, 2004).

As with any statistical analysis, the researcher should provide evidence of reliability and validity of each of the variables in the model.

Because hierarchical linear modeling is a regression-based technique, the assumptions of linear regression models continue to apply. One commonly overlooked assumption of linear regression is that the independent variables are measured reliably. When one or more predictor variables are measured with error, the results of the analysis might be misleading. The likelihood of Type II error increases for the measures that exhibit low reliability, while the likelihood of Type I error increases for the other variables in the model (for example, Osborne and Waters, 2002). Therefore, it is especially important to provide evidence of reliability of scores for all of the continuous independent variables in the model.

Conclusion

This chapter has provided a general introduction to the estimation of multilevel models and hypothesis testing in the multilevel framework. We have also provided a brief introduction to the use of model fit criteria and proportion of variance explained statistics to evaluate the adequacy of a given model. We encourage the interested reader to consult Raudenbush and Bryk (2002) for a more in-depth treatment of all of these topics; however, we hope that this primer provides some basic information on estimation and model fit issues in multilevel modeling.

References

Aiken, L. S., and West, S. G. *Multiple Regression: Testing and Interpreting Interactions.* Newbury Park, Calif.: Sage, 1991.
Biesanz, J. C., and others. "The Role of Coding Time in Estimating and Interpreting Growth Curve Models." *Psychological Methods,* 2004, *9,* 30–52.
Bozdogan, H. "Model Selection and Akaike's Information Criterion (AIC): The General Theory and Its Analytical Extensions." *Psychometrika,* 1987, *52,* 345–370.
Burnham, K. P., and Anderson, D. R. "Multimodel Inference: Understanding AIC and BIC in Model Selection." *Sociological Methods and Research,* 2004, *33,* 261–304.
Cohen, J., Cohen, P., West, S. G., and Aiken, L. S. *Applied Multiple Regression/Correlation Analysis for the Behavioral Sciences.* (3rd ed.). Mahwah, N.J.: Lawrence Erlbaum Associates, 2003.
de Leeuw, J. "Multilevel Analysis: Techniques and Applications (Book Review)." *Journal of Educational Measurement,* 2004, *41,* 73–77.
Enders, C. K., and Tofighi, D. "Centering Predictor Variables in Cross-Sectional Multilevel Models: A New Look at an Old Issue." *Psychological Methods,* 2007, *12,* 121–138.
Gelman, A., and Pardoe, I. "Bayesian Measure of Explained Variance and Pooling in Multilevel (Hierarchical) Models." *Technometrics,* 2006, *48*(2), 241–251.
Kline, R. B. *Principles and Practice of Structural Equation Modeling.* (2nd ed.). New York: Guilford Press, 2005.
Myung, J. "A Tutorial on Maximum Likelihood Estimation." *Journal of Mathematical Psychology,* 2003, *47,* 90–100.
Osborne, J. W., and Waters, E. "Four Assumptions of Multiple Regression that Researchers Should Always Test." *Practical Assessment, Research and Evaluation,* 2002, *8*(2). Retrieved May 13, 2011, from http://PAREonline.net/getvn.asp?v = 8&n = 2.

Raftery, A. E. "Bayesian Model Selection in Social Research." *Sociological Methodology,* 1995, *25,* 111–163.

Raudenbush, S. W., and Bryk, A. S. *Hierarchical Linear Models: Applications and Data Analysis Methods.* (2nd ed.). Thousand Oaks, Calif.: Sage Publications, 2002.

Raudenbush, S. W., Bryk, A., Cheong, Y. F., and Congdon, R. T. *HLM 6: Hierarchical Linear and Nonlinear Modeling.* Chicago: SSI, 2004.

Roberts, J. K., Monaco, J. P., Stovall, H., and Foster, V. "Explained Variance in Multilevel Models." In J. J. Hox and J. K. Roberts (eds.), *Handbook of Advanced Multilevel Analysis.* New York: Routledge, 2011.

Schwarz, G. "Estimating the Dimension of a Model." *Annals of Statistics,* 1978, *6,* 461–464.

Singer, J. D., and Willett, J. B. *Applied Longitudinal Data Analysis: Modeling Change and Event Occurrence.* New York: Oxford University Press, 2003.

Snijders, T. A., and Bosker, R. J. "Modeled Variance in Two-Level Models." *Sociological Methods and Research,* 1994, *22,* 342–363.

Snijders, T. A., and Bosker, R. J. *Multilevel Analysis.* Thousand Oaks, Calif.: Sage Publications, 1999.

Verbeke, G., and Molenberghs, G. *Linear Mixed Models for Longitudinal Data.* New York: Springer-Verlag, 2000.

Wagenmakers, E., and Farrell, S. "AIC Model Selection Using Akaike Weights." *Psychonomic Bulletin and Review,* 2004, *11,* 192–196.

Weakliem, D. L. "Introduction to the Special Issue on Model Selection." *Sociological Methods and Research,* 2004, *33,* 167–187.

Zucchini, W. "An Introduction to Model Selection." *Journal of Mathematical Psychology,* 2000, *44,* 41–61.

D. BETSY MCCOACH is an associate professor in the measurement, evaluation, and assessment program at the University of Connecticut.

ANNE C. BLACK is an associate research scientist in the department of psychiatry at Yale University.

3

Multilevel modeling is becoming a very popular method of estimating models where participants are nested within groups. It allows researchers to estimate models where independence is an assumption—an assumption that may not be tenable. This chapter examines the data sources available and the software used to estimate multilevel models.

Using Existing Data Sources/Programs and Multilevel Modeling Techniques for Questions in Institutional Research

Joe P. King, José M. Hernandez, Joe L. Lott, II

Multilevel modeling (MLM) gives researchers the ability to make inferences about organizations where nesting factors will bias results and the assumption of independence is not tenable. This chapter provides an overview of the variety of data sources that lend themselves to conducting institutional research (IR). It not only serves as a repository of data ready for use (although some have restrictions), it gives a blueprint on how secondary data sets are designed and maintained. The latter part of the chapter gives an overview of the software that runs multilevel models. There are many more software programs than those listed here; we describe some of the more widely used ones.

Data Sources for Multilevel Modeling

This section provides institutional researchers with a guide to data sources and structures that lend themselves to a multilevel analysis. Nested data are very common in higher education, as a combination of public, private, and institutional data has been used to construct IR studies (Pascarella and Terenzini, 2005). These data tend to have large sample sizes and a robust set of variables that describe individual-level and group-level sample characteristics. A robust set of variables within a large data set

NEW DIRECTIONS FOR INSTITUTIONAL RESEARCH, no. 154, Summer 2012 © Wiley Periodicals, Inc.
Published online in Wiley Online Library (wileyonlinelibrary.com) • DOI: 10.1002/ir.20013

allows the researcher to explore a complex set of research questions (Gelman and Hill, 2007). Of course, it is the researcher's responsibility to make sure that the data being used are appropriate for the types of questions that will be analyzed (Thomas and Heck, 2001).

Many examples in research journals have applied multilevel techniques to their data to understand how various elements of the college environment are correlated with intended outcomes. Studies have investigated the impact of campus diversity on the academic achievement of students (Pascarella and others, 2006; Cole, 2007), the impact of student social networks on campus on the academic success of students (Chang, Denson, Saenz, and Misa, 2006; Rhee, 2008), and the impact of parental involvement on the enrollment patterns of students post high school (Perna and Titus, 2005). Studies have also focused on the relationship between college quality and how it affects student outcomes in the form of employment and earning opportunities (Thomas, 2000, 2003; Zhang, 2005). MLM allows a researcher to investigate the correlational relationships between group-level and individual-level variables, where the group-level variables are products of the nesting structure of the data, as is the case when a researcher is interested in comparing student outcomes between public and private schools on standardized tests (National Center for Education Statistics, 2006). Similarly, Strauss and Volkwein (2004) utilized student-level variables of overall impression, satisfaction, and sense of belonging to understand and compare the varying levels of institutional commitment between two- and four-year colleges. These types of analyses provide a greater understanding of how effective higher education institutions are in achieving individual institutional goals while also accounting for student-level variation.

Public Data Sources. As stated previously, researchers have used public, private, and institutional data sources, each with varying levels of availability (some license requirements may apply), for IR. Public data are collected from government institutions and are available based on certain conditions. At the federal level, data from the National Center for Education Statistics (NCES; see Table 3.1 for a partial list of studies) and the National Science Foundation (NSF; see Table 3.2 for a similar list) are two of the most widely utilized public data resources to understand the impact of educational institutional contexts on a range of outcomes using MLM techniques. These entities have data from a number of longitudinal and cross-sectional studies. The process for acquiring these data can vary by the study, and they are publicly available. There are complete lists of all postsecondary data sets (Survey and Programs, n.d.) and more information on how to acquire a restricted data set (Publications and Products, n.d.).

Private Data. Organizations also collect data from both private and public institutions. Researchers interested in accessing these data usually have to pay a fee and/or submit a research proposal detailing the nature of

NEW DIRECTIONS FOR INSTITUTIONAL RESEARCH • DOI: 10.1002/ir

Table 3.1. Partial List of NCES Surveys

NCES Surveys	Description
Integrated Postsecondary Education Data System (IPEDS) http://nces.ed.gov/ipeds/	Gathers information on every college, university, and technical/vocational institution that participates in the federal student aid program. This survey provides basic data to explore trends in terms of number of students enrolled, staff employment numbers, financial information, and degree attainment.
Baccalaureate and Beyond (B&B) http://nces.ed.gov/surveys/b%26b	Includes students who completed their bachelor's degree and explores the participation of recent baccalaureate recipients in the workforce and other activities. Also explores income and debt trends of recent graduates.
Beginning Postsecondary Students (BPS) http://nces.ed.gov/surveys/bps/	First-time students enrolled at a higher education institution for undergraduate studies. Includes variables exploring persistence/attrition and completion of first-time undergraduates, financial aid, and a variety of student variables.
National Postsecondary Student Aid Study http://www.nces.ed.gov/surveys/npsas/	Provides information about student financial aid from all possible sources, and explores the variables associated with retention as it relates to financial aid.
National Study of Postsecondary Faculty http://www.nces.ed.gov/surveys/nsopf/	Nationally representative sample of full and part-time faculty of public and private not-for-profit two- to four-year institutions. Includes variables that explore intuitional trends associated with hiring, departures, tenure policies, etc.
High School and Beyond http://nces.ed.gov/surveys/hsb/	Longitudinal variables following students from their senior year in high school up until employment after college.

the study. Typically the information submitted includes the problem statement, research questions, variables of interest, and methodological approach. One of the most widely used sources of private data comes from the Cooperative Institutional Research Program (CIRP) administered by the Higher Education Research Institute (HERI), which is located at the University of California at Los Angeles. Established in 1966, CIRP is the oldest empirical study of higher education that involves data from over 1,900 institutions and over 15 million students (Higher Education Research Institute, n.d.). HERI administers several CIRP surveys yearly, including the Freshman Survey, Your First College Year, Diverse Learning Environments, College Senior Survey, and HERI Faculty Survey (HERI,

Table 3.2. Partial List of NSF Studies

NSF Surveys	Description
Survey of Earned Doctorates (SED) http://www.nsf.gov/statistics/ srvydoctorates/	Yearly data of all research doctorates awarded by U.S. institutions. Explores trends in doctoral degree completion by field, with demographic, educational history, and future plans variables, to name a few.
National Survey of Recent College Graduates (NSRCG) http://www.nsf.gov/statistics/ srvyrecentgrads/	This is a cross-sectional survey that explores the degree attainment of science and engineering college graduates.
National Survey of College Graduates (NSCG) http://www.nsf.gov/statistics/ srvygrads/	Data provide information on the number of individuals educated or employed in science and engineering fields.
Survey of Graduate Students and Postdoctorates in Science and Engineering (GSS) http://www.nsf.gov/statistics/ srvygradpostdoc/	Data on graduate enrollment, postdoctoral positions, and doctoral nonfaculty research employment by department. Also explores trends on graduate enrollment in science, engineering, and health fields.

CIRP Surveys and Services, n.d.). Researchers have used CIRP data to examine diversity, climate perception levels by student, and the extent to which different institutions address diversity issues (Wood and Sherman, 2001; Chang, Denson, Saenz, and Misa, 2006; Rhee, 2008). They also have used HERI data to explore degree attainment rates and the relationships between a variety of campus climate conditions at different colleges and universities across the United States (Astin and Oseguera, 2005; Oseguera and Rhee, 2009). Furthermore, researchers have used the Faculty Survey data to explore faculty member mentoring practices in science, technology, engineering, and math (STEM) and a variety of other fields (Sax, Bryant and Harper, 2005; Eagan and others, 2011).

Similarly, the National Survey of Student Engagement (NSSE) at the University of Indiana provides important student engagement data. In particular, such data provide unique insights about the quality of collegiate experiences by collecting information on the amount of time and effort students dedicate to their educational experiences. NSSE data also include information about how institutional resources are allocated toward activities linked to student learning (Bringle and Hatcher, 1996; Kuh, 2003). NSSE surveys both students and faculty from hundreds of four-year colleges and universities about student participation in programs and activities provided by their own institutions for the purposes of learning and personal development. These data have been used to examine the role that diversity plays in enhancing student educational experiences and how positive educational experiences are associated with retention and persistence (Pike, 2006; Umbach and Kuh, 2006). More generally, these data can be used to examine "successful" trends and practices utilized by different institutions to ensure student success (Pascarella and others, 2006; Laird and Cruce, 2009). In most of the studies that utilize NSSE data, students are nested units within different institutions across the United States. For instance, a researcher can easily examine the impact of university first-year seminars on student persistence across different institutions using NSSE (Porter and Swing, 2006).

Institutional Data. Institutional data provide information on students, faculty and staff, and other departmental and administrative units for the purpose of strategic planning and resource management. More specifically, information on college diversity, enrollment, student retention, tuition disbursements, major classification of students, and budgeting plans are readily available from these data. Institutional data also play a key role in the decision process that occurs internally within institutions. For example, the University of Washington's Office of Educational Assessment provides data and tools for institutional assessment, departmental assessment, and course-based assessment. Most of the data collected are geared toward improving student experiences and include information about student engagement, library use, campus climate, use of technology, and drug and alcohol use, to name a few. Since the data are organized across the different disciplines, they are ideal for MLM approaches in which students and staff are nested within departmental units (see http://www.washington.edu/oea/assessment/institutional.html). Institutional data are perhaps the most readily available data to researchers and yet the most underutilized in IR. In many cases, obtaining these data does not require user licenses, and most campuses are interested only in what their own internal researchers are investigating. For example, a study in which a researcher interested in investigating the persistence of minority student populations in relation to the level of engagement at a given campus in the state of Florida can use NSSE data in conjunction with the Florida Department of Education Student Database to determine what influences the desired outcomes (Greene, Marti, and McClenney, 2008). Furthermore, if a researcher is interested in the relationship among student socioeconomic status, financial aid distribution, and degree attainment outcomes that are nested within different majors, his or her home institution's own data would suffice to develop a methodologically sound study.

Considerations when Applying MLM to Large-Scale Data Sets

Data Access. After determining which data source is most appropriate for multilevel analysis, many issues with accessing the data must be considered. One of the most convenient ways to access data is to retrieve them through some online medium where the data can be directly imported into an input file. NCES has a few studies that allow users to access data online; one is the National Educational Longitudinal Study (http://nces.ed.gov/surveys/nels88/), and another is the Postsecondary Education Quick Information System (http://nces.ed.gov/surveys/peqis/).

Some entities require a restricted license to access their data. Acquiring such a license usually requires an individual to write a proposal to the organization that owns the data. The proposal typically describes the nature of the research, lists the research questions, and describes how the data will be used to answer those questions. Access to the data will have several contingencies, depending on the granting entity. These contingencies may include securing the data, nondisclosure agreements, and other precautionary measures. If dealing with medical information, researchers must consider special actions under the Health Insurance Portability and Accountability Act (1996).

Sampling Designs. Sampling designs have implications for data collection, data quality, and the generalizability of results. The researcher must clearly understand the data structure and the units that correspond to each clustering level; ignoring the sampling design will present challenges to researchers when making inferences from the sample data to the larger population. For example, the Baccalaureate and Beyond methodology report provides information on the requirements for both target populations of students (those who received a baccalaureate degree) and the population of eligible institutions (Wine and others, 2004). Obtaining and exploring methodology reports of the data that will be utilized in a study will ensure that the researcher is familiar with the data structure. In cases where methodology reports are not available, the researcher should contact the organization or institution that owns the data for more information.

Variable Naming Across Waves. On average, data sets utilized for IR contain thousands of variables representing different aspects of the survey. For example, a data set might contain information on student characteristics, parent information, and institutional variables. Another difficulty may be data that consist of multiple waves of data at varying time points. Although not explicit, most data sets will have a unique identifier for each type of variable to help researchers decipher what will be relevant for their particular research questions. For example, variables found in a data set that consists of data taken at four different time points are labeled according to the corresponding year (Student Socioeconomic status [SES] in 1994, 1997, 2000, 2003 = B1STSES, B2STSES, B3STSES, B4STSES; where B1 corresponds to 1994, B2 corresponds to 1997, and so on, and ST corresponds to "student" variable). Because the naming convention of variables will vary by data set, it is important for researchers to consult the code book to ensure that they understand the labels.

Relevance of Data. One of the limitations of using secondary data is that often the data were not collected with the purpose of the current research in mind. Therefore, researchers must have a thorough understanding of the data source and the utility of the variables in answering their research questions. The quality of the data is a very important issue; the greater the quality of the data, the more confident researchers can be in their conclusions. Quality of data encompasses many aspects, such as sample size, amount of missing data, and whether groups of interest are well sampled (that is, whether minority groups are proportionally sampled). In many cases, researchers may have to recode, manipulate, or change the nature of the variables, which may include standardizing variables and creating composites, among other things. Disproportionate sampling can be aided by weights, which will give proper weights to different groups so better conclusions can be drawn. A combination of theory, extant literature, and thorough descriptive analyses provides the best guides about variable construction.

Another issue to consider is the types of variables used in model building. Continuous variables, which assume an underlying continuity, may give better results than categorical variables. One example of this is income. Specific income figures, instead of a polytomous variable that groups income levels, lower misidentification of the different income categories. The appealing aspect of a continuous variable is it can be categorized when necessary.

Software to Estimate Multilevel Models

A number of software applications are appropriate to estimate multilevel models, with the programs ranging from very user-friendly to more complex. Academic disciplines and institutions vary regarding the type of software that is utilized, and many times choice is based on familiarity, licensing fees, and professional standards. Next we discuss some of the commonly used software for multilevel analysis in the social sciences.

HLM. HLM is a program based on a graphical user interface (GUI) that can handle many multilevel models and is controlled by a point-and-click mechanism. This program has a wide variety of abilities and estimation procedures. It can fit models with different outcomes that have different distributions, such as those that are continuous, nominal, ordinal, or count data. It also can apply weights to the parameter estimates. In addition, it automatically imputes missing data within level-one files (Raudenbush and Bryk, 2002; Raudenbush, Bryk, Cheong, and Congdon, 2004). Many studies have reported using HLM software in their analysis (http://www.ssicentral.com/hlm/index.html).

Benefits. HLM is a very user-friendly program that walks the data analyst through the process of setting up the file needed for modeling. The GUI interface makes it efficient for people to create a multilevel model and specify the model(s) they want to run. A file is created that saves the model information, such as the data being used, the variables, and model specification. This allows researchers to return to the model to run additional analysis on the data. There are many specifications for different types of estimation procedures, with different types of outcomes. HLM has a detailed user guide that demonstrates how to model different types of outcomes (Raudenbush and Bryk, 2002; Raudenbush, Bryk, Cheong, and Congdon, 2004). Support is available to individuals who purchase the software.

Challenges. HLM has limitations on the models it will run. The software cannot estimate more uncommon models, such as zero inflated count models (models where the outcome is a nonnegative integer with more zeros than the model expects). In addition, many of the default options may not be appropriate for each model so it is best for users to understand what the default options are. HLM relies on SPSS, SAS, STATA, SYSTAT, or free format (a text file) for its residuals. HLM does not have a mechanism to analyze model residuals, therefore another statistical program is needed, such as SPSS, SAS, STATA, R, or even Excel; this could be an obstacle if a researcher does not have access to these and other analysis programs (Raudenbush, Bryk, Cheong, and Congdon, 2004).

SPSS. SPSS is a GUI program used for data analysis in a wide variety of fields. It is relatively flexible and can perform functions from data cleaning and manipulation to data analysis. SPSS is very user-friendly because of its extensive documentation; user manuals and books provide code for the models (for example, Stevens, 2009). It uses a point-and-click method of data analysis instead of command line interfaces like other statistical programs. Although users can manipulate the statistical methods by altering the underlying syntax, in most cases doing so is not necessary. SPSS also has methods using mixed models to run multilevel models through its base program. It is very popular for advanced statisticians as well as beginning students (Field, 2009; SPSS Inc., 2010).

Benefits. One of the very strong options of this package is its data manipulation and recoding abilities, as SPSS has the ability to recode variables within the same variable or into a different variable and it has many recoding algorithms, which gives great flexibility to a researcher. SPSS also has many add-on packages that can implement many types of models, including more advanced missing data imputation, structural equation modeling (through AMOS), creating tables, bootstrapping, complex surveys, and others (see SPSS web site at http://www-01.ibm.com/software/analytics/spss/products/statistics/). It also has some powerful graphing abilities and a separate add-on for users to create better tables for data viewing and publication. SPSS is in wide use, and many books are based on it (Field, 2009; Norusis and SPSS Inc., 2011; Leech, Barrett, and Morgan, 2011); it also is used outside academia. Its strong help file assists users to learn program functions. Finally, the program's most recent update added the ability to analyze nonlinear outcomes (version 19; SPSS Inc., 2010).

Challenges. Some more uncommon models may not be able to be estimated. Currently, the only outcomes that can be estimated are linear (normally distributed) outcomes, binomial, multinomial, and count data. SPSS also can use the gamma and inverse Gaussian distributions. Other models, such as those with zero inflated counts or models of ordered data, cannot be estimated in a multilevel context in SPSS (SPSS Inc., 2010). In addition, some of the defaults may not be known; users should be familiar with how the program estimates the model to ensure it is working properly.

Mplus. Mplus is a syntax-based program (a program that relies on text commands rather than point and click) that has the ability to estimate many types of models, including latent variable models, regression, path analysis, multilevel, and Bayesian models. This program can specify a diverse range of models and has fine control over the models; it also has many options for output, which allows researchers to see the estimates that go into the analysis (such as a correlation or covariance matrix). In addition, the program will export output into data files that can be read from a spreadsheet or word processing program, which gives MPlus extraordinary flexibility in allowing researchers to use the model that best fits the data and the analysis (Muthén and Muthén, 1998–2010).

Benefits. Mplus is a very flexible program that can model many types of outcomes; the output is thorough; and researchers can specify the types of statistics reported in the output. The ability to write syntax allows researchers to know exactly what model is being specified. One benefit of all syntax programs is that the syntax can be saved for future use. If a similar model is being analyzed, much of coding is already done, and only minor changes must be made. The output of MPlus is robust in the statistics it produces, and it gives researchers a deep understanding of how well the model is fitted and the relationships between variables. This function can assist in model selection, model diagnostics, and other issues. Finally, error statements tend to be quite specific on what went wrong with the model, enabling researchers to determine whether the error is in the code or in the model they are attempting to estimate.

Challenges. Mplus is a syntax-based program; for that reason, it is not as easy as GUI-based programs, which means more time investment to ensure the syntax is running the right model. A lengthy learning curve may be needed to learn a syntax-based program. In addition, different models require different specifications in different parts of the code, as there are places to specify variables, the type of analysis, and types of models.

One challenge of Mplus is how the data file is read into the program. Most statistics programs read in a data file and look at the first row of the data as the variable names and the second row as the start of the data. In Mplus, no variable names can be used in the first row; the data begin there. The variable names are listed in the syntax in the order in which they are in the data file. Naming variables in the syntax file can be daunting with larger data files. Many programs, such as SPSS and HLM, take variable names from the first row.

SAS. SAS is a well-known statistical package that uses programming rather than a GUI interface. It comes with prepackaged functions to implement different models and a detailed user manual (SAS Institute Inc., 2009). The SAS program can implement both linear and nonlinear models. The user manual provides a brief introduction to the models it estimates and coding language. Several published books provide SAS code to implement the models (Der and Everitt, 2008; Stevens, 2009).

Benefits. SAS can analyze a wide range of outcome variables, including linear models, generalized linear models, and nonlinear models (such as growth curve models). The package is very flexible and can be used for many types of models and can answer a wide range of research questions that may not be possible with more limited programs. SAS is also very widely used; therefore, understanding this program will be advantageous when working with other scholars and people outside academia.

Challenges. SAS is a syntax-based program, and users must learn the command language. As with all syntax programs, the code to specify models in this program is not the same as other programs, such as Mplus. Researchers will have to know how to specify the model based on this program's syntax because there is no universally accepted coding scheme for programs. Books such as those by Stevens (2009) give coding details for SAS, as does the program manual (SAS Institute Inc., 2009).

R. R is an open source programming language that supports a vast array of statistical models (R Development Core Team, 2010). This program is freely available online and actively updated. There are hundreds of additional packages, including additional functions to the base package. In addition, people can create and add their own packages for personal use or use among other R users via an online repository. MLM is done widely in a package called lme4, which can handle many types of outcomes, such as linear, binary, and count. The package MCMCglmm implements Monte Carlo Markov chains to estimate multilevel models; it has all the options available to lme4 plus many more families of models (Hadfield, 2010).

Benefits. R is extraordinarily flexible. It has the ability to use built-in functions (miniprograms within R to carry out specific tasks or computations) and to create functions or code to implement specific models using matrix formulations or calculations. In addition, if no function exists, users can write the code themselves to estimate the parameters of their model. Doing so is laborious and requires a detailed understanding of how to estimate the model, including using R commands to run the code.

Unlike many open source programs, R has extensive documentation from other researchers. Many books have been written on R for MLM (Gelman and Hill, 2007). A book series called *Use R!* is published by Springer (http://www.springer.com/series/6991), and John Wiley & Sons has a number of "Featured Titles in Statistics Using R" (http://www.wiley .com/WileyCDA/Section/id-302388.html).

Challenges. R does not come with a language generator, as Mplus does, or heavy documentation, as SAS does. Because it is open source, there is no technical support available to individuals other than mailing lists. As with other syntax-based programs, learning all the functions can be quite challenging, and a lot of practice is required to understand and implement the language proficiently.

The decision on what program to use should be based on a few criteria. The main criterion is what kind of models will be estimated. Some programs may not be able to handle very complex models. Researchers who are going to be running a diverse group of models should know several packages of software or a software package that can estimate many types of models.

Programs to Assist in Analysis

Programs are available that help get data ready before primary data analysis. Many times researchers have to "clean" the data before they are ready for multilevel analysis. Doing this includes creating composite variables and recoding values that are missing for different reasons (for instance, a data set may have one code for a valid nonresponse and another for failure to respond). For purposes of analysis, it may help to code all codes for missing values into one missing value variable. Other common and necessary steps to get data ready to analyze include recoding variables, such as taking the logarithm, changing continuous variables into categories, and recoding categorical string variables (in other words, characters only, not numbers) into numbers.

Excel. Microsoft Excel is a widely distributed spreadsheet program. This program is not a statistical analysis package but a spreadsheet that can do a multitude of tasks. However, a statistical package can be downloaded from the Microsoft web site (http://office.microsoft.com/en-us/ excel-help/load-the-analysis-toolpak-HP001127724.aspx; Microsoft Corporation, 2010) that will do basic statistical testing (but not advanced testing such as multilevel models). Excel is appropriate for some preliminary tasks that are necessary before data analysis can occur. It is excellent at importing multiple file types, such as comma-separated values (CSV) or tab-delineated values (TAB). These types of data files make it flexible to be read by many programs and to visualize the data in a spreadsheet format. Manipulating the data is easy. If an institution does not have access to Excel, an open source version of a spreadsheet called Openoffice.org includes the tools necessary for data manipulation and cleaning but may not have the statistical tools available in Excel.

Stat/Transfer. The Stat/Transfer program solves a major issue regarding transferring data to different programs. File formats that use CSV, TAB, or space-separated values are common, but SPSS and SAS use proprietary formats. Researchers using SPSS can export the data in a format that can be read nearly universally. Researchers who do not have access to proprietary programs can use a program like Stat Transfer (Circle Systems, 2009). Also researchers can take files that are already in CSV or TAB format and turn them into SPSS or SAS files, which may help if importing into those programs is not working well. Stat Transfer includes many types of formats, allowing a researcher to convert a data set from one program to another.

Dealing with Missing Data

One very common problem in social research is missing values in the data, which could complicate data analysis. Missing data can strongly affect results, especially when the missing data are not random (see Schafer and Graham, 2002, for more information).

Listwise Deletion. One of the simpler yet statistically indefensible techniques of the treatment of missing data is listwise deletion of data. When the variables are placed in the model, if there is one missing data point in the data matrix, the entire case is deleted by the statistical software (Schafer and Graham, 2002). The listwise deletion process only analyzes cases where responses to all variables in the data set are available. (More information is available at Rubin, 1987, 1996; Schafer and Graham, 2002.)

Imputation Approaches. The data that are present can be used to predict what the missing values will take. The most common method is the EM Algorithm (Rubin, 1987, 1996). Running missing data imputation can add complexity to fitting the model (although programs are making this less of a problem) but can add strength to the conclusions of the analysis.

Multiple imputation is easy to implement in Mplus and HLM by stating, in the command file, that there are missing data. Mplus and HLM programs will automatically impute the missing data and then run the analysis on the full amount of data they were able to compute. SPSS has separate packages for multiple imputation, although other imputation is done in its base software package. With this external package, users can create imputed data sets and run the analysis on them as well through the program's missing values add-on (http://www-01.ibm.com/software/analytics/spss/products/statistics/missing-values/features.html?S_CMP=rnav). SAS also can run multiple imputation in its many analyses; it will impute data sets and combine the data sets into one data set that can be analyzed using rules set by Rubin (1987).

Final Thoughts

This chapter presents an overview of the data sources and software that facilitate multilevel model estimations. A plethora of data sets are available, both publicly downloadable and restricted yet usable by qualified researchers. These data sources can make answering substantive research questions easier by allowing for analysis of data already collected, which includes dealing with the challenging, ever-present problem of missing data. Finally, we discuss software for fitting multilevel models. The technology is advancing so rapidly that this software will get significantly better as time progresses and as more advanced models are developed.

References

Astin, A. W., and Oseguera, L. *Degree Attainment Rates at American Colleges and Universities.* Higher Education Research Institute, University of California, Los Angeles, 2005.

Bringle, R. G., and Hatcher, J. A. "Implementing Service Learning in Higher Education." *Journal of Higher Education,* 1996, 67(2), 221–239.

Chang, M. J., Denson, N., Saenz, V., and Misa, K. "The Educational Benefits of Sustaining Cross-Racial Interaction among Undergraduates." *Journal of Higher Education,* 2006, 77(3), 430–455.

Circle Systems. Stat/Transfer. [Computer Software]. Seattle, Wash.: Circle Systems, 2009.

Cole, D. "Does Interracial Matter? An Examination of Student-Faculty Contact and Intellectual Self-Concept." *Journal of Higher Education,* 2007, 78(3), 249–281.

Der, G., and Everitt, B. S. *A Handbook of Statistical Analyses Using SAS.* (3rd ed.). Boca Raton, Fla.: Chapman and Hall/CRC, 2008.

Eagan, M., and others. "Engaging Undergraduates in Science Research: Not Just About Faculty Willingness." *Research in Higher Education,* 2011, 52(2), 151–177.

Field, A. *Discovering Statistics Using SPSS (Introducing Statistical Methods).* Thousand Oaks, Calif.: Sage Publications, 2009.

Gelman, A., and Hill, J. *Data Analysis Using Regression and Multilevel/Hierarchical Models.* New York: Cambridge University Press, 2007.

Greene, T. G., Marti, C. N., and McClenney, K. "The Effort-Outcome Gap: Differences for African American and Hispanic Community College Students in Student Engagement and Academic Achievement." *Journal of Higher Education,* 2008, 79(5), 513–539.

Hadfield, J. D. "MCMC Methods for Multi-Response Generalized Linear Mixed Models: The MCMCglmm R Package." *Journal of Statistical Software,,* 2010, 33(2), 1–22.

Health Insurance Portability and Accountability Act (HIPAA) of 1996. Pub. L. No. 104–191, 110 Stat. 1936, 1996.

HERI, CIRP Surveys and Services. n.d. Retrieved July 20, 2011, from http://www.heri.ucla.edu/herisurveys.php.

Higher Education Research Institute. "About CIRP." n.d. Retrieved July 20, 2011, from http://www.heri.ucla.edu/abtcirp.php.

Kuh, G. D. "What We're Learning About Student Engagement from NSSE: Benchmarks for Effective Educational Practices." *Change,* 2003, 35(2), 24–32.

Laird, T.F.N., and Cruce, T. M. "Individual and Environmental Effects of Part-Time Enrollment Status on Student-Faculty Interaction and Self-Reported Gains." *Journal of Higher Education,* 2009, 80(3), 290–314.

Leech, N. L., Barrett, K. C., and Morgan, G. A. *SPSS for Introductory and Intermediate Statistics: IBM SPSS for Intermediate Statistics: Use and Interpretation.* (4th ed.). New York: Routledge Academic, 2011.

Microsoft Corporation. Microsoft Office. [Computer Software]. Redmond, Wash.: Microsoft Corporation, 2010.

Muthén, L. K., and Muthén, B. O. *Mplus User's Guide.* (6th ed.). Los Angeles: Muthén and Muthén, 1998–2010.

National Center for Education Statistics. *Comparing Private Schools and Public Schools Using Hierarchical Linear Modeling.* Washington, D.C.: United States Dept. of Education, National Center for Education Statistics, 2006.

Norusis, M., and SPSS, Inc. *IBM SPSS Statistics 19 Advanced Statistical Procedures Companion.* Reading, Mass.: Addison-Wesley, 2011.

Oseguera, L., and Rhee, B. S. "The Influence of Institutional Retention Climates on Student Persistence to Degree Completion: A Multilevel Approach." *Research in Higher Education,* 2009, *50*(6), 546–569.

Pascarella, E. T., and Terenzini, P. T. *How College Affects Students.* San Francisco: Jossey-Bass, 2005.

Pascarella, E. T., and others. "Institutional Selectivity and Good Practices in Undergraduate Education: How Strong Is the Link?" *Journal of Higher Education,* 2006, *77*(2), 251–285.

Perna, L. W., and Titus, M. A. "The Relationship between Parental Involvement as Social Capital and College Enrollment: An Examination of Racial/Ethnic Group Differences." *Journal of Higher Education,* 2005, *76*(5), 485–518.

Pike, G. R. "Students' Personality Types, Intended Majors, and College Expectations: Further Evidence Concerning Psychological and Sociological Interpretations of Holland's Theory." *Research in Higher Education,* 2006, *47*(7), 801–822.

Porter, S., and Swing, R. "Understanding How First-Year Seminars Affect Persistence." *Research in Higher Education,* 2006, *47*(1), 89–109.

Publications and Products. n.d. Retrieved July 20, 2011, from http://nces.ed.gov/pub search/licenses.asp.

R Development Core Team. *R: A Language and Environment for Statistical Computing.* Vienna, Austria: R Foundation for Statistical Computing, 2010.

Raudenbush, S. W., and Bryk, A. S. *Hierarchical Linear Models: Applications and Data Analysis Methods.* (2nd ed.). Thousand Oaks, Calif.: Sage Publications, 2002.

Raudenbush, S. W., Bryk, A. S, Cheong, Y. F., and Congdon, R. *HLM 6 for Windows.* [Computer software]. Lincolnwood, Ill.: Scientific Software International, Inc, 2004.

Rhee, B. S. "Institutional Climate and Student Departure: A Multinomial Multilevel Modeling Approach." *Review of Higher Education,* 2008, *31*(2), 161–184.

Rubin, D. B. *Multiple Imputation for Nonresponse in Surveys.* New York: John Wiley & Sons, 1987.

Rubin, D. B. "Multiple Imputation After 18+ Years." *Journal of the American Statistical Association,* 1996, *91*(434), 473–489.

SAS Institute Inc. *SAS/STAT® 9.2 User's Guide.* (2nd ed.). Cary, N.C.: SAS Institute Inc, 2009.

Sax, L. J., Bryant, A. N., and Harper, C. E. "The Differential Effects of Student-Faculty Interaction on College Outcomes for Women and Men." *Journal of College Student Development,* 2005, *46*(6), 642–657.

Schafer, J. L., and Graham, J. W. "Missing Data: Our View of the State of the Art." *Psychological Methods,* 2002, *77*(2), 147–177.

SPSS Inc. *IBM SPSS Statistics 19 Core System User's Guide.* Chicago: SPSS Inc., 2010.

Stevens, J. P. *Applied Multivariate Statistics for the Social Sciences.* (5th ed.). New York: Routledge Academic, 2009.

Strauss, L. C., and Volkwein, J. F. "Predictors of Student Commitment at Two-Year and Four-Year Institutions." *Journal of Higher Education,* 2004, *75*(2), 203–227.

Survey and Programs. n.d. Retrieved July 20, 2011, from http://nces.ed.gov/ surveys/SurveyGroups.asp?group = 2.

Thomas, S. "Deferred Costs and Economic Returns to College Quality, Major, and Academic Performance: An Analysis of Recent Graduates in Baccalaureate & Beyond." *Research in Higher Education*, 2000, *41*(3), 281–313.

Thomas, S. "Longer-Term Economic Effects of College Selectivity and Control." *Research in Higher Education*, 2003, *44*(3), 263–299.

Thomas, S. L., and Heck, R. H. "Analysis of Large-Scale Secondary Data in Higher Education Research: Potential Perils Associated with Complex Sampling Designs." *Research in Higher Education*, 2001, *42*, 517–540.

Umbach, P. D., and Kuh, G. D. "Student Experiences with Diversity at Liberal Arts Colleges: Another Claim for Distinctiveness." *Journal of Higher Education*, 2006, *77*(1), 169–192.

Wine, J., and others. *1993/03 Baccalaureate and Beyond Longitudinal Study (BandB:93/03) Field Test Methodology Report* (NCES 2004–02). Washington, DC: National Center for Education Statistics, 2004.

Wood, T. E., and Sherman, M. J. "Is Campus Racial Diversity Correlated with Educational Benefits?" *Academic Questions*, 2001, *14*(3), 72–88.

Zhang, L. " 'Do Measures of College Quality Matter?': The Effect of College Quality on Graduates' Earnings." *Review of Higher Education*, 2005, *28*(4), 571–596.

Joe P. King is a fourth-year doctoral student in educational psychology at the University of Washington, Seattle.

José M Hernandez is a second-year doctoral student in educational leadership and policy studies at the University of Washington, Seattle.

Joe L. Lott, II, is an assistant professor in educational leadership and policy studies at the University of Washington, Seattle.

4

This chapter discusses multilevel models for binary outcomes. Models for categorical data analysis and their multilevel extensions have been used extensively in biostatistics, psychometrics, sociology, and economics but are used somewhat less in other branches of the behavioral and social sciences. After a brief overview of models for binary data and a discussion of multilevel models, two example analyses on institutional data are presented.

Multilevel Models for Binary Data

Daniel A. Powers

Regression models for the analysis of categorical data are relatively recent additions to the methodological toolbox when compared to traditional linear models. Multilevel models for categorical outcomes have a much shorter history. Although there is considerable literature and a long history on the methods for categorical data analysis dating at least back to the early 1900s, the most rapid development of specific techniques for modeling categorical data occurred over the past several decades. The most rigorous development of these methods occurred in economics (Maddala, 1983; Amemiya, 1991), statistics (Fineberg, 1980; Agresti, 2002), and sociology (Long, 1997; Powers and Xie, 2008).

The methods and models for categorical data analysis cover considerable ground, ranging from regression-type models for binary and binomial data, count data, to ordered and unordered polytomous variables, as well as regression models that mix qualitative and continuous data. I focus here on methods for binary or binomial data, which are perhaps the most widely applied models in categorical data analysis and may be the most relevant for institutional research where predictions such as program participation, graduation, or dropout are particularly relevant. These particular categorical models are also the most fully developed in the literature on multilevel models.

This chapter is organized as follows: I provide a brief overview of two of the most important models for categorical data analysis to show how these models are adapted to the multilevel or mixed modeling framework using the generalized linear mixed model. I then examine a simple model

NEW DIRECTIONS FOR INSTITUTIONAL RESEARCH, no. 154, Summer 2012 © Wiley Periodicals, Inc.
Published online in Wiley Online Library (wileyonlinelibrary.com) • DOI: 10.1002/ir.20014

of program placement from both the conventional modeling and then multilevel perspectives. Finally, I consider a more ambitious multilevel analysis of program dropout.

Modeling Categorical Outcomes

A categorical outcome is inherently distinct from a continuously measured outcome insofar as the value of the outcome has no intrinsic meaning with regard to location and scale of some measure. For example, the typical binary response variable, Y, is coded as 0 or 1, with 1 generally representing the presence of a particular attribute. This differs from a continuous measure in that the measured distance between the response values of 0 or 1 is not quantifiable to the extent that it would be in the case of continuous variables, where the difference in measurements reflects a meaningful magnitude. Given this indeterminacy in the location and scale of the outcome variable, models for binary dependent variables generally focus on modeling probability functions or transformations of probability functions. In contrast to the treatment of continuous outcomes, the outcome of interest is not the particular value of the binary variable (0 or 1) but rather a function of the probability that Y assumes a particular value. More formally, one can model probability functions of Y, that is, $\Pr(Y_i = 1)$. In the binary regression context, where X_i denotes a set of predictors for the ith observation, interest centers on modeling a transformation of the probability that $Y = 1$ conditional on the values of X.

Overview of Common Models for Binary and Binomial Responses

Individual-level data are usually characterized by a binary response. However, it is possible to aggregate the individual binary responses such that Y represents a count of the number of successes in n independent Bernoulli trials, each of which is characterized by a 0 or 1 outcome. This is the familiar coin-tossing idea of obtaining five heads in ten tosses. Assume for now that we have individual binary data on a random sample of n individuals. The standard models assume that these observations are independent and identically distributed, which is referred to as the independent and identically distributed (or "i.i.d.") assumption. We revisit this assumption later when dealing with multilevel data. As mentioned earlier, we are interested in modeling the probability of $Y = 1$. A realistic model must ensure that predicted probabilities lie in the [0,1] interval. A common method to ensure this is through a nonlinear transformation of the probability function. Relatively straightforward transformations are derived from basic principles of mathematical statistics. For example, the Z-score can be viewed as mapping the cumulative probability to the real line. Suppose that $p = F(z) = \Pr(Z \leq z) = \Phi(z)$ denotes the probability of observing a value in a standard normal distribution less than or equal to z, then the inverse function $\Phi(p)^{-1} = z$ is a transformation of that probability to the z scale. Thus, the nonlinear probability scale is linearized by a "stretching" transformation $\Phi(p)^{-1} = z$. Because z values are unbounded, it makes sense to cast the linear model on this scale rather than on the probability scale to avoid out-of-bounds predictions as well as to take advantage of the desirable asymptotic properties of the transformed variable. The probit model (where the dependent measure can take only one of two variables—male or female, for example) results from this specification. The logit transformation is also widely used. In this case, the natural logarithm of the odds of $Y = 1$ yields a value of z that is unbounded. The odds may be expressed as $p/(1 - p)$. The "logit" transformation $z = \log[p/(1-p)]$ can be inverted to yield the cumulative probability $p = F(z) = \Pr(Z \leq z) = e^z/(1 + e^z)$. Note that due to symmetry of the logistic and normal distributions $\Pr(Z \leq z) = \Pr(Z \geq -z)$. These results form the basis of the logit model. The mapping of the relation between $F(z)$ and z for the probit and logit models is shown in Figure 4.1.

We can see that the logistic distribution has somewhat thicker tails, owing to its larger variance when compared to that of the standard normal distribution. However, this distinction is of little practical consequence when choosing a statistical model. The logit model is often preferred on the grounds that the estimated coefficients have the convenient

Figure 4.1. Mapping z to the Cumulative Probability $F(z)$

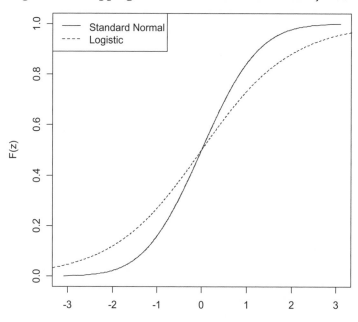

interpretation of raising or lowering the log odds of $Y = 1$. For example, a logit model may be written using the earlier notation:

$$\text{logit}(p_i) = \alpha + \beta X_i, \tag{1}$$

where X denotes a set of independent variables (or predictors) and α and β denote the constant term (intercept) and a set of regression coefficients, respectively. Then α represents the baseline log odds (or logit) of $Y = 1$ when $X_i = 0$, and β quantifies the change in the logit corresponding to a unit change in X. Thus, the interpretation on the logit scale is analogous to the interpretation of the linear regression, yielding the so-called generalized linear model (GLM; McCullagh and Nelder, 1989). It is often of interest to quantify the magnitude of the odds in one group relative to the odds in another group in a logit model. In this case, e^β quantifies the increase in the odds of $Y = 1$ for a unit change in X.

Some traditions—most notably in economics and psychology—prefer to cast binary response models in terms of the latent continuous variable Y^*, in which case a standard model is:

$$Y_i^* = \alpha + \beta X_i + \varepsilon_i, \tag{2}$$

where ε is either a standard normal or standard logistic variable. Due to the indeterminacy of the scale of the latent variable Y^*, the random errors are assumed to be distributed with a mean of 0 and a fixed variance. The variance of ε is fixed at 1 for the probit model and at $\pi^2/3$ for the logit model. Fixing the residual variance in this manner has implications for hierarchical models for binary responses. In particular, the level-one variances are fixed known quantities and thus are not estimated.

Multilevel Models for Categorical Outcomes

Multilevel or clustered data consist of units of analysis at a lower level nested within units of analysis at a higher level. Goldstein (2003) considers these hierarchies of units of analysis to be natural, insofar as there is a tendency for individuals within a particular hierarchy to be more alike in their characteristics than a similar sample of individuals chosen at random from the population. Families are a good example of a natural hierarchy because we would expect children of the same parents to be similar in many important ways. Students nested in schools would be another typical hierarchical data structure. Often hierarchies reflect individual social differentiation, for example, when individuals of similar ability are grouped in selective schools. In other cases, nesting may be less reflective of individual characteristics and may arise effectively at random. For example, in clinical research, we often find experimental trials conducted at several randomly chosen hospitals or among randomly selected groups of individuals.

NEW DIRECTIONS FOR INSTITUTIONAL RESEARCH • DOI: 10.1002/ir

Clustered Data. A clustered (or hierarchical) data structure allows a model to be formulated at different levels of analysis than would be possible if the hierarchical structure were ignored. For example, suppose we are interested in the relationship between students' family backgrounds and students' academic performances measured by passing a standardized test. Not only can we have a student-level analysis, but we can also study the relationship at the school level comparing school-level outcomes, such as the proportion of students passing a standardized test, by students' average family background within a school. For the latter school-level analysis, we would construct variables from the aggregation of the individual-level measures on students. Sampling could take place at the school and student levels, with trade-offs made in terms of the number of schools to be sampled and the number of students from each school to be sampled to maximize statistical power for multilevel analyses, which depends on both the substantive research question and the nature of the data to be collected. The higher-level units of analysis—schools in our example—are called level-two data, while the lower-level units of analysis—students in our example—are called level-one data. The focus in this chapter is mainly on the level-one data structure.

Repeated Measures or Longitudinal Data. For the clustered data just discussed, we considered sampling individuals at level one and schools or families at level two. When repeated measurements are made on the same individuals, a hierarchy is established with individuals at level two and measurement occasions at level one. These data are often referred to simply as longitudinal data. It is important to distinguish between longitudinal designs with repeated data on the same subjects (a panel design) and trend studies consisting of repeated cross-sections of different samples of individuals. The models just described can be extended to model data that are not independent due to being nested in, or allocated to, various higher-level units or contexts. The key to the difference, as with clustered data in general, is the dependence among the repeated measures on the same subject. The models for clustered data considered here will consist of two levels or hierarchies. Extension to more than two levels is straightforward. There are a number of excellent resources for learning more about these methods: Longford (1993); Kreft and de Leeuw (1998); Snijders and Bosker (1999); Hox (2002); Raudenbush and Bryk (2002); Goldstein (2003); and Skrondal and Rabe-Hesketh (2004). An excellent repository of material can be found at http://www.mlwin.com/links/materials.shtml.

Models that take advantage of these features of the data are known variously as random effects models, random coefficients models, multilevel models, hierarchical models, growth-curve models, and mixed models. The literature on linear mixed models (also called hierarchical linear models) dates back several decades. These models are widely applied to the study of longitudinal change in the form of growth-curve models and have a long history in educational research, where they are used to examine school effects and cross-context relationships involving individual-level and school-level variables. Two complementary goals of multilevel analysis are to model cross-level effects and to improve on classical (that is, maximum likelihood) estimates of within-context effects (Wong and Mason, 1985).

Multilevel models for binary data have gained widespread popularity in the social sciences in recent years due to the increasing availability of suitable data, advances in computing hardware and software, and persistent social science interest in modeling categorical outcomes. For a review of recent sociological applications, see Guo and Zhao (2000). These models have a somewhat longer history in psychometrics and biometrics (Rasch, 1961; Stiratelli, Laird, and Ware, 1984). Econometricians have also made important contributions to the literature, particularly in relation to discrete choice models, in recent decades (for example, Train, 2003). Advances in computing have expanded the menu of options available to researchers wishing to estimate models for multilevel categorical data. Models based on numerical methods that were considered computationally expensive a decade ago are now feasible and continue to be added to standard software packages. Agresti, Booth, Hobert, and Caffo (2000) discuss applications of generalized mixed models that build on the foundations of the generalized linear model as well as competing estimation approaches. Hierarchical methods have a long history in Bayesian analysis. Advances in computation have made these methods feasible, and the advent of user-friendly software is helping to popularize this approach.

As noted earlier, it is often useful to think of carrying out inferences at each level of analysis. For example, consider school-level data, with students nested in schools. Viewed this way, schools are a random sample from the population of all schools, and students are a random sample of individuals from those schools. Most treatments of hierarchical models follow the random effects approach, in which there is stochastic variation in responses at the individual level and/or group level. For random effects binary response models, the random error of the level-two units is the stochastic component of primary interest. As with the single-level binary response models considered earlier, the variance of the level-one units is fixed due to the inherent lack of scale associated with categorical dependent variables. Parameters that do not vary stochastically are sometimes called fixed-effects (Raudenbush and Bryk, 2002); these are referred to here as fixed coefficients to avoid confusion with a different use of the term *fixed-effects*, which refers to the fixed-effects approach to estimating models for clustered or longitudinal data. In the fixed-effects approach, inference is based on level-one data after conditioning on a sample of level-two units. The fixed-effects model statistically controls for the fixed differences across level-two units of analysis.

NEW DIRECTIONS FOR INSTITUTIONAL RESEARCH • DOI: 10.1002/ir

Models for Clustered Binary Data

Before investigating random effects models, we need to adopt some notational conventions to distinguish among the various levels of analysis in hierarchical models. Following Hedeker and Gibbons (2006), let us assume that there are N level-two units with n_i level-one units in the ith cluster yielding a total sample size of:

$$n = \sum_{i=1}^{N} n_i. \tag{3}$$

A logit model with a random intercept at level-two is a natural starting point for investigation. This specification is similar in spirit to the generalized linear model but is referred to as a generalized linear mixed model (GLMM) to highlight its hierarchical structure.

$$\text{logit}(p_{ij}) = \alpha + \beta X_i + u_i \tag{4}$$

Here p_{ij} denotes the response probability $\Pr(Y_{ij} = 1)$ for the jth individual from the ith cluster. As in the standard model, we have included X to account for observed sources of variation in the logit. The level-two residual u_i is assumed to be normally distributed with mean 0 and variance σ_u^2 and independent of X. (The normal and multivariate normal distribution for random effects is used because extensions to more than one random effect are mathematically tractable compared to other distributions.) Conditional on X, the random effect u_i increases the expected responses for all individuals in cluster i when it is positive and decreases those individuals' expected responses when it is negative. In this sense, u_i can be viewed as contributing to the probability that $Y_{ij} = 1$, or in terms of affecting the latent Y_{ij}^*, with $\Pr(Y_{ij} = 1) = \Pr(Y_{ij}^* > 0)$. When the response pattern for the binary dependent variable is modeled using a logit model, as in Equation 4, we refer to the resulting generalized linear mixed model as a logistic-normal mixture model.

It is instructive to express this model in another way that highlights the idea of a randomly varying intercept. Equation 4 is referred to as the within-cluster formulation. We could just as easily define the model at each of the two sublevels. Suppose, for example, that X varies by institutions and Z varies among individuals within institutions.

$$\text{logit}(p_{ij}) = \beta_{0i} + \beta_1 Z_{ij}$$
$$\beta_{0i} = \beta_{00} + \beta_{01} X_i + u_i \tag{5}$$

This setup makes it clear that the random intercept β_{0i} varies among level-two units, with a mean of β_{00}, which represents the mean of the intercept of the level-two units conditional on X. We note that the institution-specific variable X affects the random intercept. By including this term in the model, we anticipate that it accounts for a portion of the institution-level variation in the intercept. The variable Z enters into the level-one submodel. Like the standard binary response models considered earlier, the residual variance is fixed at $\pi^2/3$ for the logit model and at 1 for the probit model. Therefore, there is no random error appearing in the level-one submodel. This means that it is not straightforward to gauge the impact of Z on the level-one variance. In fact, including covariates at level one tends to increase the level-two variance, as it effectively reduces the residual variance at level one, which is fixed by the scale normalization that characterizes binary response models.

It is important to note that the interpretation of the estimates from a random coefficients model differs from that of a fixed coefficients model, which is a model that does not contain a random component at level two but otherwise looks similar to the random coefficient model. Coefficients from the random-coefficients logit (or logistic-normal) model refer to log odds ratios that are conditional on the random components at level two and therefore have a cluster-specific interpretation. In contrast, the estimates from the fixed-coefficients model are population average estimates, reflecting the average effects over the population of level-one units. This distinction between conditional effects and marginal effects can be confusing, but it well illustrates the point that inferences can be carried out at two levels of analysis.

Example 1: Modeling Postdoctoral Placement. The next example uses a data set consisting of forty Ph.D.-granting institutions with information on the number, Y, of postdoctoral placements in biochemistry departments with n students (for example, see Allison, 1987). We assume that within any university (a level-two unit), level-one units (Ph.D. students) are exchangeable insofar as the data contain no individual-level information about these students, so that those sharing the same level-two context cannot be distinguished from one another. Had the individual-level data been collected, it would have been possible to further differentiate students on the basis of their observed characteristics.

Suppose that the goal is to evaluate the probability of placement into postdoctoral training. We might begin by examining the placement probabilities for each of the forty universities. Perhaps the most straightforward approach would be to use the maximum likelihood estimator $\hat{p}_i = Y_i/n_i$ to estimate each home institution's probability of placing a student in a postdoctoral position at a host institution. Figure 4.2 shows the estimated placement probabilities and their 95 percent confidence intervals. We can see that not only is there considerable variation between universities in the placement probabilities, but that these estimates exhibit notable differences in precision, as illustrated by the variability in the widths of the confidence intervals for estimates of roughly the same magnitude. The

Figure 4.2. Estimated Probability of Postdoctoral Placement (Maximum Likelihood Estimates) and 95 Percent Confidence Intervals

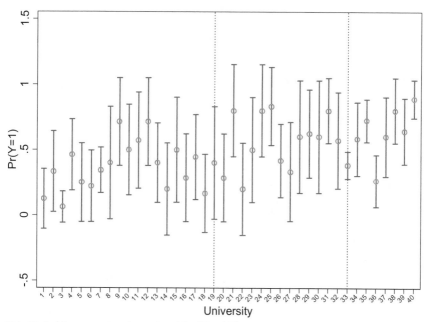

Note: Dotted lines correspond to universities 19 and 33.

precision of each estimate is determined by the magnitude of the estimate and the sample size. For example, university 19 has an estimated placement probability of 0.40 based on a sample of five students whereas university 33 has an estimate of 0.38 based on a sample of eighty-six students. Despite the similarity in these two point estimates, the standard error of the estimate for university 19 is over four times that of university 33 at 0.22 and 0.05, respectively.

Maximum likelihood estimates are known to be unbiased in large samples. However, some of the estimates shown in Figure 4.2 are based on samples as small as five and suffer from some imprecision as a consequence. How could a model improve on these estimates? The estimates just given are obtained by considering each university independently of all the others. This is tantamount to estimating fixed effects of postdoctoral placement, for example, by fitting a regression with a constant term and thirty-nine dummy variables in a standard logit model. If we consider these forty institutions to be drawn from a larger population of institutions, we can obtain an alternative estimate of the probability of postdoctoral placement. For example, a single-level model:

$$\text{logit}(p_i) = \alpha, \tag{6}$$

provides the overall (or pooled) estimator of the postdoctoral placement probability as:

$$p = e^{\alpha}/(1 + e^{\alpha}). \tag{7}$$

The pooled estimator is a constant and effectively ignores the inter-institution variability in postdoctoral placement. However, a multilevel model with a university-specific random effect will allow for this variation around the population average:

$$\begin{aligned}\text{logit}(p_i) &= \alpha_i \\ &= \alpha + u_i,\end{aligned} \tag{8}$$

where u follows a normal distribution with mean 0 and variance σ_u^2. This expression makes it clear that each university-specific logit (α_i) is equal to the population average logit (α) plus a university-specific residual (u_i). The individual-level prediction would therefore be specified as:

$$p_i = e^{\alpha + u_i}/(1 + e^{\alpha + u_i}), \tag{9}$$

which now varies across institutions. The population average would now be conditional on the random effects:

$$p_i = \int_u e^{\alpha + u_i}/(1 + e^{\alpha + u_i}) g(u)du, \tag{10}$$

where $g(u)$ denotes the normal density function pertaining to the random effect u. Thus we see that the population average represents individual predictions that are averaged over the random effects distribution. If there is interinstitution variation in the random effects, this population average would be different from the marginal probability estimated in Equation 7. We can see from Figure 4.3 that the individual estimates from the multi-level model (denoted by triangles) differ from the maximum likelihood estimates (denoted by circles) to the extent that they are shrunken toward the overall mean and have smaller sampling variances as indicated by their narrower confidence intervals.

More precise estimates exhibit little shrinkage, whereas less precise estimates experience considerably more. The multilevel estimates thus represent a trade-off or compromise between the unbiased maximum like-lihood estimates in favor of a biased estimate with lower mean square error. The multilevel estimates are "improved" in the sense that they bor-row information from the other units in the sample and regard the sample as a proper subset of a population of level-two units as opposed to treating each level-two unit as an isolated fixed entity without regard to a wider population of level-two units.

Figure 4.3. Estimated Probability of Postdoctoral Placement

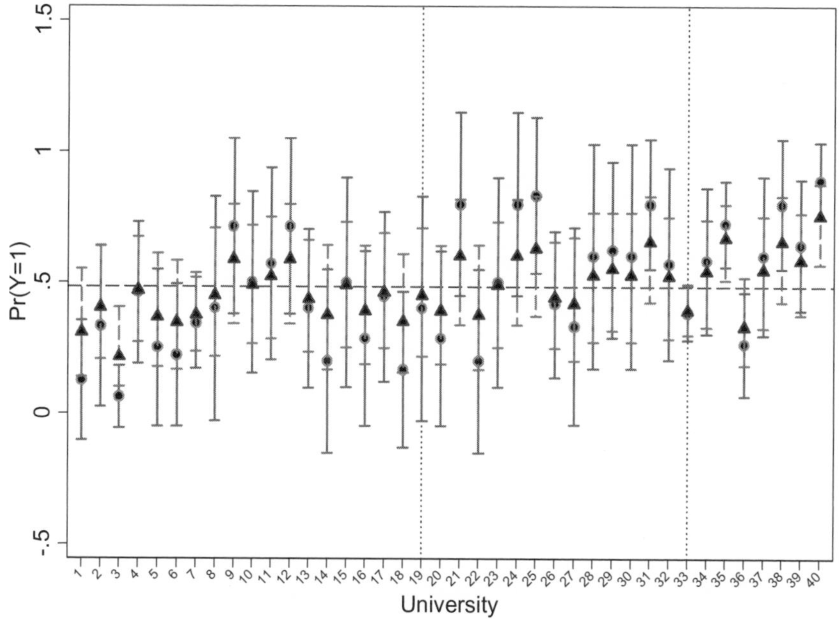

Note: The ML estimates are denoted by circle, and the multilevel estimates are denoted by a triangle. The 95 percent confidence intervals around each estimate are shown. Dotted lines correspond to universities 19 and 33. The dashed line denotes the population average postdoctoral placement probability of 0.484.

Comparison of Statistical Models of Postdoctoral Placement. Table 4.1 compares the results from the model of Equation 6 with those of Equation 7. Model 1 is a special case of Model 2 with the constraint $\sigma_u^2 = 0$. Because these models are estimated using maximum likelihood and differ by a single parameter σ_u^2, we can use likelihood ratio tests to gauge improvement in fit from one model to the next. In this case, the likelihood ratio χ^2 value of $634.72 - 615.86 = 18.9$ on one degree of freedom is statistically significant ($p < 0.0001$). Most statistical routines report the asymptotic standard error of σ_u^2, which is generally available as a by-product of the optimization procedure.

We see that when conditioning on the unmeasured institution-specific factors represented by u, the estimate of the intercept is attenuated. This is to be expected as there is considerable variation around the average logit of -0.076 and there are several institutions with large random effects. Figure 4.4 shows the magnitude of random effects (Panel a) with the empirical distribution (Panel b) for the forty institutions. The estimated random effects shown in Figure 4.4 are the empirical Bayes (or expected a posteriori) estimates of u. That is, they are obtained by

**Figure 4.4. Estimated Random Effects for Forty
Institutions (a) and Their Distribution (b)**

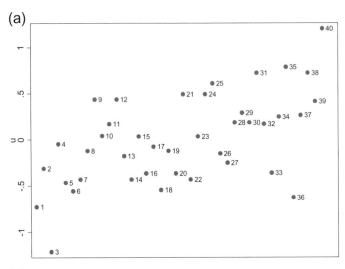

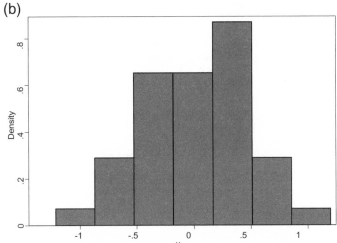

**Table 4.1. Estimates and Standard Errors Standard and
Multilevel Model**

	Model 1		Model 2	
	Estimate	*Std. Error*	*Estimate*	*Std. Error*
Intercept	−0.118	0.094	−0.076	0.159
σ_u^2	—	—	0.497	0.227
log L	634.72		615.86	

combining prior information about the distribution of u along with sample information. These estimates were obtained by evaluating the next conditional expectation:

$$\hat{u}_i = E(u_i \,|\, Y_i) = \frac{\int_u u_i \ell(Y_i \,|\, u_i) g(u)du}{\int_u \ell(Y_i \,|\, u_i) g(u)du}, \tag{11}$$

where $\ell(Y_i|u_i)$ denotes the conditional likelihood on the data for the ith institution and $g(u)$ is the standard univariate normal density function. This expression must be evaluated numerically but is generally available as a by-product of estimation.

Many, if not most, problems in institutional research involve the analysis of individual-level data as opposed to the aggregated data used in the previous example, which assumed exchangeability of individuals within clusters and therefore did not use information from the level-one units. To provide a more complete picture of a typical multilevel analysis, we consider a data set consisting of roughly 3,600 graduate students who entered various Ph.D. programs at a major research university in the southern United States. Lott, Gardner, and Powers (2009) originally used these data in an event-history analysis of Ph.D. program dropout. Here we ignore the dynamic-temporal aspect of the data and simply look at the odds of dropping out of the program that was originally entered. The relevant hierarchical aspect of these data is the nesting of students in specific academic programs (majors). We argue that these social and academic contexts create a natural dependency in the outcomes for the students within them. Here, as in the original paper, we focus on the students who originally entered twenty-five science, technology, engineering, and math (STEM) programs.

Example 2: Modeling Program Dropout. As an example, we examine the probability of program dropout for graduate students who entered Ph.D. programs at a large university between 1984 and 1999. About 47 percent of students entering graduate programs during this period failed to complete the program they had originally entered. Following Lott, Gardner, and Powers (2009), we examine the effects of several individual-level and context-level predictors.

Data for Study. A combination of sociodemographic and institutional structure variables were utilized in a multivariate analysis, including race, sex, age, marital status, and citizenship. Race is coded as five dummy variables pertaining to non-Hispanic white, non-Hispanic black, Hispanic, Asian, and unknown race/ethnicity, with white/unknown as the reference category. Sex is coded 1 for female, 0 otherwise. Marital Status is coded 1 = married and 0 for nonmarried. Citizenship is a categorical variable that listed the codes of the particular country of citizenship for each individual in the data set. This variable is coded 0 for non-U.S. citizens and 1 for U.S.

Table 4.2. Descriptive Statistics

	Percent
Female	25.3%
% Female in Program	30.5%
White	62.3%
Black	5.3%
Latino	4.6%
Asian	27.8%
U.S. Citizen	45.5%
% U.S. Citizen in Program	46.8%
Married	21.0%

	Mean	Std. Dev.	Min.	Max.
Age	28.7	5.8	19	76
GRE/100	11.6	1.6	5.3	16.0
Relative GRE	1.0	0.1	0.5	1.4

$N = 3,598$

citizens. GRE is the combined verbal and quantitative score and is rescaled to 100-point intervals. Table 4.2 provides descriptive statistics on these and other measures.

Major as a Context. It is safe to say that a particular program may impart certain attributes on a student. That is, graduate students are influenced by the social contexts of their particular programs. Departments differ in curricula requirements, admissions criteria, financial support, and requirements for degree completion. These different departmental characteristics are shaped by disciplinary norms and practices (Golde, 1998), many of which are formalized and codified in specific department policies. Other aspects of programs are less visible. For our particular data, all of these attributes are unmeasured, and it is reasonable to argue that these factors affect the risk of dropout. In particular, the unmeasured characteristics of a specific program can affect completion and dropout beyond the effects of the measured characteristics alone. Rather than including all twenty-five program-specific constants as fixed effects, we assume a normally distributed random effect for program in a generalized linear mixed model, with students (at level one) nested in programs (at level two). The program random effect serves to raise or lower the baseline log odds of dropping out for a student in that program, conditional on, and in addition to, his or her observed characteristics as well as the observed characteristics of that program. Accounting for the random effect of program means that the effects of individual-level and program-specific

NEW DIRECTIONS FOR INSTITUTIONAL RESEARCH • DOI: 10.1002/ir

predictors must be interpreted as being conditional on, or adjusted for, unmeasured program-specific characteristics.

We consider students in twenty-five STEM programs with a total of 3,598 students. The number of students per program ranges from 31 to 369. We include two program-specific (level-two) measures: percentage female and percentage of U.S. citizens in the program. We include an absolute measure of the GRE score scaled by dividing by 100. Additionally, we compute a relative GRE measure that reflects an individual's departure from the program average in the relative sense. An interesting picture of the GRE effect is obtained from an examination of relative GRE. That is, the absolute measure of GRE may be tapping a different dimension than would a measure that reflects a departure (in a relative sense) from a program's average GRE score. An absolute measure likely captures a global propensity for success in graduate school, while a relative-to-program measure may tap the program-specific propensity for success. A relative GRE greater than 1.0 indicates a higher GRE score relative to one's peers in the program; a relative GRE lower than 1.0 indicates a lower GRE score relative to the program average. Relative GRE ranges from 0.49 (51 percent lower GRE score than average in the program) to 1.45 (45 percent higher GRE than the average in the program).

Table 4.3 shows the results of three models fit to these data, the conventional logit model (Model 1), a random effects logit containing a random intercept (Model 2), and a random coefficients model containing a random intercept along with a program-varying effect of U.S. citizenship (Model 3). The effects of the remaining predictors are assumed to be fixed (not varying by major). Equation 12 shows the form of Model 2 and Model 3 as a GLMM with a vector of fixed effects ($\boldsymbol{\beta}$) and random effects ($\mathbf{u}$), and $\mathbf{x}$ and $\mathbf{z}$ are the respective vectors pertaining to these effects.

$$\text{logit}(p_{ij}) = \mathbf{x}'_{ij}\boldsymbol{\beta} + \mathbf{z}'_{ij}\mathbf{u}_i \qquad (12)$$

In this case, $\mathbf{u}$ consists of a random intercept and a random slope denoted by u_0 and u_1, respectively. These are assumed to be normally distributed with means 0 and covariance matrix Σ_u, the diagonal elements of which are the variances of u_0 and u_1 and the off-diagonal is the covariance between them, that is,

$$\Sigma_u = \begin{bmatrix} \sigma_0^2 & \sigma_{01} \\ \sigma_{01} & \sigma_1^2 \end{bmatrix}.$$

Estimates of the fixed effects are in the form of odds ratios (OR). The notable effects are that older age, a higher percentage of females in the major, a higher percentage of U.S. citizens in the program, being Hispanic, being married, and having a higher GRE score than one's peers in the

Table 4.3. **Multivariate Models of Program Dropout**

Fixed Effects	Model 1		Model 2		Model 3	
	OR	Z	OR	Z	OR	Z
Age	0.98	−3.24	0.98	−2.98	0.98	−3.09
Female	1.15	1.93	1.16	1.71	1.15	1.67
% Female (major)	0.93	−0.06	0.64	−0.54	0.60	−0.69
Black	1.25	0.62	1.22	1.17	1.27	1.40
Hispanic	0.77	−1.79	0.78	−1.38	0.79	−1.28
Asian	1.23	2.31	1.24	2.24	1.23	2.13
U.S. Citizen	1.21	2.57	1.22	2.21	1.24	1.74
% U.S. Citizen (major)	0.12	−5.50	0.15	−3.15	0.16	−3.47
Married	0.73	−4.06	0.74	−3.22	0.74	−3.16
GRE	1.72	5.91	1.56	3.62	1.54	4.03
Relative GRE	0.01	−4.17	0.02	−2.72	0.02	−2.96

Variance Components						
σ_0^2	—		0.11		0.22	
σ_{01}	—		—		−0.16	
σ_1^2	—		—		0.14	
Log L	−2326.9		−2308.7		−2303.4	
LR test		36.29		10.62		
$N = 3,598$		$df = 1$		$df = 2$		

Note: OR = Odds Ratio.

program are all negatively predictive of dropping out. Most interesting, we note that a 100-point increase in GRE increases the odds of dropout by 54 percent (Model 3). As alluded to earlier, this measure may be best viewed as a global measure of propensity for success in graduate school and may be less predictive of success in a particular program. Relative GRE may better tap the success potential in a particular context and may be the preferred measure in this case. Hierarchically structured data allow the possibility to incorporate variables that are "centered" in substantively meaningful ways around their context means, and are thus able to capture additional key dimensions of interest in institutional research. Figure 4.5 evaluates the estimated GRE effect together with the protective effect of relative GRE at the average value of GRE and illustrates the utility of considering both the absolute and relative measures together. We find, for example, that the odds of dropping out are over three times those of remaining in the program for a student with a GRE score equal to the program's mean GRE score. This translates to a dropout probability of 0.77. However, a 31 percent increase in this student's GRE score above the program's average would render the odds of dropout equal to the odds of

Figure 4.5. The Effect of Relative GRE Evaluated at the Sample Average GRE Score

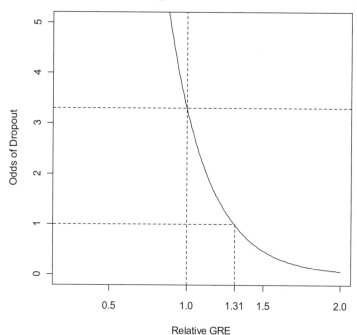

remaining in the program (a dropout probability of 0.50, or equal odds). Moreover, we find that the likelihood of retention is vastly improved as the relative GRE exceeds about 1.3.

Interpreting Variance Components. Model 2 includes the variance component for the random intercept. The one degree of freedom likelihood ratio test indicates that this model provides a significant improvement in fit with the additional variance parameter relative to Model 1 ($\chi^2_{(1)} = 36.3$, $p < 0.001$). Including the additional variance components associated with the U.S. citizenship in Model 3 provides a modest improvement over Model 2 ($\chi^2_{(2)} = 10.6$, $p < 0.002$). The covariance between the randomly varying intercept and U.S. citizen effect is negative (in other words, the larger the program-specific effect of U.S. citizenship the lower the odds of dropout), as illustrated in Figure 4.6. The correlation between the random effects is −0.91. Figure 4.6 shows the association between the random coefficients.

Summary

This chapter provides an overview of multilevel models for binary outcomes with two applications. The empirical examples are especially

Figure 4.6. Association between the Random Intercept and the Random Slope of U.S. Citizenship

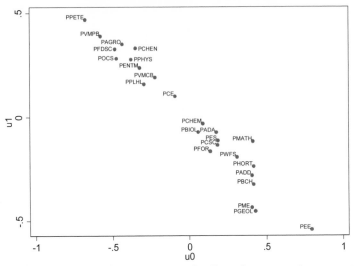

Note: This figure indicates that large program-specific effects of U.S. citizenship are associated with lower odds of dropout. Acronyms in figure refer to graduate programs.

relevant to questions involving binary outcomes, which are increasingly commonplace in institutional research settings. These methods are readily extended to events occurring in time (see, for example Chapters 5 and 6 in Powers and Xie, 2008; Lott, Gardner, and Powers, 2009) and to longitudinal data (see, for example, Hedeker and Gibbons, 2006). More detailed development of these methods can be found elsewhere (for example, Raudenbush and Bryk, 2002; Skrondal and Rabe-Hesketh, 2004).

References

Agresti, A. *Categorical Data Analysis*. (2nd ed.). Hoboken, N.J.: John Wiley & Sons, 2002.

Agresti A., Booth, J. C., Hobert, J. P., and Caffo, B. "Random-Effects Modeling of Categorical Response Data." *Sociological Methodology*, 2000, *30*, 27–80.

Allison, P. D. "Introducing a Disturbance into Logit and Probit Regression Models." *Sociological Methods and Research*, 1987, *15*, 355–374.

Amemiya, T. "Qualitative Response Models: A Survey." *Journal of Economic Literature*, 1991, *19*, 483–536.

Fineberg, S. E. *The Analysis of Cross-Classified Categorical Data*. (2nd ed.). Cambridge, Mass.: MIT Press, 1980.

Golde, C. M. "Beginning Graduate School: Explaining First-year Doctoral Attrition." In M. S. Anderson (ed.), *The Experience of Being in Graduate School: An Exploration*. San Francisco: Jossey-Bass, 1998.

Goldstein, H. I. *Multilevel Statistical Models*. (3rd ed.). London: Edward Arnold, 2003.

Guo, G., and Zhao, H. "Multilevel Modeling for Binary Data." *Annual Review of Sociology,* 2000, *26,* 441–462.

Hedeker, D., and Gibbons, R. D. *Longitudinal Data Analysis.* Hoboken, N.J.: John Wiley & Sons, 2006.

Hox, J. *Multilevel Analysis: Techniques and Applications.* Mahwah, N.J.: Lawrence Erlbaum Associates, 2002.

Kreft, I., and de Leeuw, J. *Introducing Multilevel Modeling.* Thousand Oaks, Calif.: Sage Publications, 1998.

Long, J. S. *Regression Models for Categorical and Limited Dependent Variables.* Thousand Oaks, Calif.: Sage Publications, 1997.

Longford, N. *Random Coefficient Models.* New York: Oxford University Press, 1993.

Lott, J. L., Gardner, S., and Powers, D. A. "Doctoral Student Attrition in the STEM Fields: An Exploratory Event-History Analysis." *Journal of College Student Retention Research, Theory and Practice,* 2009, *11,* 247–266.

Maddala, G. S. *Limited-Dependent and Qualitative Variables in Econometrics.* Cambridge: Cambridge University Press, 1983.

McCullagh, P., and Nelder, J. A. *Generalized Linear Models.* (2nd ed.). New York: Chapman and Hall, 1989.

Powers, D. A., and Xie, Y. *Statistical Methods for Categorical Data Analysis.* (2nd ed.). London: Emerald, 2008.

Rasch, G. "On General Laws and the Meaning of Measurement in Psychology." *Proceedings of the 4th Berkeley Symposium on Mathematical Statistics and Probability,* 1961, *4,* 321–333.

Raudenbush, S. W., and Bryk, A. S. *Hierarchical Linear Models: Applications and Data Analysis Methods.* (2nd ed.). Thousand Oaks, Calif.: Sage Publications, 2002.

Skrondal, A., and Rabe-Hesketh, S. *Generalized Latent Variable Modeling: Multilevel and Longitudinal, and Structural Equation Models.* London: Chapman Hall, 2004.

Snijders, T. B., and Bosker, R. J. *Multilevel Analysis: An Introduction to Basic and Advanced Multilevel Modeling.* Thousand Oaks, Calif.: Sage Publications, 1999.

Stiratelli, R., Laird, N., and Ware, J. H. "Random Effects Models for Serial Observations with Binary Response." *Biometrics,* 1984, *40,* 961–971.

Train, K. *Discrete Choice Methods with Simulation.* Cambridge: Cambridge University Press, 2003.

Wong, G. Y., and Mason, W. M. "The Hierarchical Logistic Regression Model for Multilevel Analysis." *Journal of the American Statistical Society,* 1985, *80,* 513–524.

DANIEL A. POWERS *is professor of sociology and faculty associate in the Division of Statistics and Scientific Computation and the Population Research Center at the University of Texas at Austin.*

5

This chapter provides an example of how cross-classified random effects modeling can be used in institutional research by examining faculty gender pay gaps overall and by principal activity.

Cross-Classified Random Effects Models in Institutional Research

Laura E. Meyers

Multilevel modeling offers researchers a rich array of tools that can be used for a variety of purposes, such as analyzing specific institutional issues, looking for macro-level trends, and helping to shape and inform educational policy. One of the more complex multilevel modeling tools available to institutional researchers is cross-classified random effect modeling (CCREM). CCREM is similar to other types of multilevel models in which people or other items of interest are nested within various categories. However, CCREM is appropriately used when the groupings of the data are not strictly hierarchical (Raudenbush and Bryk, 2002; Beretvas, 2008). For example, higher education faculty members can be nested within academic disciplines and institutions. At first glance, a three-level hierarchical model might seem appropriate because faculty members tend to affiliate with a particular discipline and that discipline may be represented within an institution. However, higher education has a more complex structure where disciplines extend across institutions (Umbach, 2009). This means that faculty members affiliated with a particular discipline are not typically located within an individual institution or institution type. CCREM can account for this type of complex data structure where faculty members are cross-classified by both discipline and institution.

This chapter provides one example of how CCREM can be used to assess faculty gender pay differentials in higher education and how those results can be used to help inform policy at the institutional level. The

NEW DIRECTIONS FOR INSTITUTIONAL RESEARCH, no. 154, Summer 2012 © Wiley Periodicals, Inc.
Published online in Wiley Online Library (wileyonlinelibrary.com) • DOI: 10.1002/ir.20015

study presented in this chapter examines the faculty gender pay gap both overall and by principal activity and describes institutional and disciplinary effects on base faculty salary. There are, however, many other powerful ways in which CCREM could be used to examine gender pay equity and help inform institutional policy. Some possibilities include: (1) estimating variance in salary between institutions, between disciplines, and between faculty; (2) estimating gender pay differentials by discipline and institution type; and (3) identifying disciplinary or institutional characteristics associated with faculty salary. For additional information about CCREM, additional examples using CCREM, and the distinction between purely nested versus cross-classified data structures, see Raudenbush and Bryk (2002) and Beretvas (2008).

Using CCREM to Understand Faculty Gender Pay and Inform Institutional Policy

Even though the Equal Pay Act and Title VII of the Civil Rights Act were passed over thirty years ago, women college faculty members still make less money than their male counterparts who have comparable affiliations and positions (American Association of University Professors, 2003–2004). Although progress has been made to equalize pay for women in academia, there is much work to be done. Several studies have examined gender pay equity issues and continue to suggest that a pay equity problem exists for women faculty in colleges and universities (Barbezat, 1989, 1991; Bellas, 1993; Toutkoushian, 1998; Perna, 2001; Toutkoushian and Conley, 2005; Umbach, 2007, 2009; Porter, Toutkoushian, and Moore, 2008). Various statistical techniques and approaches have been used to estimate the gender salary gap, such as: regressions (Toutkoushian, 1998; Perna, 2001; Toutkoushian and Conley, 2005); the Oaxaca procedure (Toutkoushian, 1998; Barbezat and Hughes, 2005); hierarchical linear modeling (Umbach, 2007; Porter, Toutkoushian, and Moore, 2008); and, more recently, CCREM (Umbach, 2009). CCREM offers institutional researchers a possibly more accurate way to examine salary equity in higher education. This type of tool can help administrators and institutional researchers gain a better understanding of the factors that contribute to the gender pay differential and more precisely focus their efforts on the areas that need the most attention.

Using data from the 2004 National Study of Postsecondary Faculty and drawing on human capital theory and structural theory, this study uses CCREM to more accurately estimate the pay differential between male and female faculty in higher education. Specifically, this study examines the faculty gender wage gap overall and by principal activity (teaching or research). This type of multilevel statistical technique is used for research designs where the data are organized by more than one level, such as faculty simultaneously nested within disciplines and institutions, and the data are not strictly hierarchical (Raudenbush and others, 2004; Beretvas, 2008; Umbach, 2009).

This study uses two theoretical approaches: human capital theory and structural theory. Researchers are just beginning to pair these theories with CCREM that takes into account the multilevel nature of higher education in which faculty are simultaneously nested within disciplines and institutions. Human capital theory uses individual characteristics and labor skills to help explain differences in rewards and salary. The theory suggests that investments in individual expertise effect current earnings and future productivity (Welch, 1975). Human capital theory and theories from labor economics suggest that "employment status is determined by an individual's productivity, the investments an individual has made in his or her productivity, and the supply of and demand of workers with similar levels and types of training and expertise" (Perna, 2001, p. 284).

One critique of human capital theory is that it does not sufficiently account for the complexities of labor markets and social structures (England, 1982; Tolbert, 1986; Perna, 2003; Umbach, 2007). Researchers consequently have sought to fill this void by incorporating structural theories into their studies (Tolbert, 1986; Perna, 2003; Umbach, 2007, 2009). Structural theorists propose that salary differentials are a result of occupational segregation, labor market partitioning, and organizational factors connected to the organization in which a worker is employed.

The two research questions that guide this study are:

1. After controlling for personal background characteristics, human capital and structural factors, what is the effect of gender on base faculty salary?
2. After controlling for personal background characteristics, human capital, and structural factors, what is the effect of gender on base faculty salary by principal activity (teaching or research)?

Methods

CCREM was selected as the method of choice for this study due to the structure of the data being studied, the nature of the research questions posed, and the ability of CCREM to potentially provide more accurate estimates of the factors and structural characteristics that may be contributing to faculty salaries. The main outcome variable for the research questions is the natural logarithm of salary. The natural logarithm of salary was used to create a more normally distributed dependent variable. Independent variables (described below) were selected based on the integrative framework derived from the literature on gender pay equity issues and rely on human capital theory and structural theory.

A general CCREM is composed of two submodels: a level-one or within-cell model and a level-two or between-cell model (Raudenbush and others, 2004). According to Raudenbush and others (2004), "The cells refer to the cross-classification by the two higher-level units" (p. 190). This study places faculty at the first level of the model and cross-classifies discipline and institution type at the second level. The level-one or within-cell model therefore represents the relationships among the faculty-level variables (individual characteristics). The level-two or between-cell model shows the influence of discipline and institutional level factors.

Multilevel modeling is often performed with a series of steps of increasing complexity. The first step of formulating and testing cross-classified random effects models is to analyze the empty, or unconditional, model (in other words, the null model) with no predictor variables (Beretvas, 2008). This allows the researcher to assess the variation in salary that exists between disciplines, between institutions, and within cells. The second step of modeling is to add predictors at each level of the model. Predictors are often added to the model in blocks.

Level-One or "Within-Cell" Model. At level one (the individual level), several human capital and demographic measures were added in blocks. The first block included an effect-coded variable for gender. The second block introduced principal activity (teaching or research) and an interaction variable between gender and principal activity. The interaction variable was created by multiplying the gender and principal activity variables together. This was done to determine whether there are significant differences in salary for male and female faculty whose principal activity is teaching or research. The third block included effect-coded variables to account for minority status, marital status, and dependent children.

The fourth block introduced several measures of human capital. These variables were grouped around measures of productivity, educational attainment, and experience. To represent productivity, total number of classes taught during the 2003 fall quarter (for credit and not for credit), career total publications and scholarly works, and percentage of time spent on instruction were used. All of these variables are continuous and were standardized using Z-scores. Because grant production is related to higher earnings (Umbach, 2009), grant production was effect-coded to represent whether a faculty member was working on a funded scholarly activity during the 2003–2004 academic year. Variables for the number of hours per week spent on unpaid professional tasks both at the institution and outside of the institution were selected because presumably more time spent on unpaid tasks may detract from the ability to devote time to paid tasks inside of the institution. These variables were also standardized to facilitate interpretation of the results.

Because investments in education are related to higher earnings (Smart, 1991), a series of variables used to represent educational attainment were effect-coded as doctorate degree, professional degree, and other degree.

Experience was measured through years of seniority in current position, years teaching in higher education, and age. Tenure status and rank are linked to differences in faculty salary. Tenure status was effect-coded as tenured, on tenure track but not yet tenured, or not on the tenure track. Rank was effect-coded as instructor or lecturer, assistant professor, associate professor, and professor. Rank is a somewhat controversial variable because of the potential for gender bias (Becker and Toutkoushian, 2003). Consequently, rank was introduced separately in the last block.

Level-Two or "Between-Cell" Model. At level two (the discipline and institution level), various structural characteristics were added to the final within-cell model to create a full model designed to determine whether there were any significant differences in salary between male and female faculty. This model included a series of effect-coded variables for institution type and discipline type to assess their effect on base faculty salary. The variables for institution type are grouped according to the 2000 Carnegie Classification System. The variables for discipline type are grouped according to traditional disciplinary categorizations: Social Sciences, Professional fields, STEM fields, Arts and Humanities, Health Sciences, and other fields.

It is important to note that although the methodological approach used in this study allows for a more accurate estimate of the disciplinary and institutional variables on faculty salaries, cross-classified random effects models can quickly become increasingly complex as factors are added to the model and data may be limited in some levels (Raudenbush and Bryk, 2002). Raudenbush and Bryk (2002) therefore suggest that researchers pay attention to the principle of parsimony and that certain covariates should be constrained. The covariates in this study were fixed, and an effort was made to select a minimal set of variables that were theoretically supported.

Data Source and Description of Study Sample

This study uses data collected from the 2004 National Study of Postsecondary Faculty (NSOPF). The NSOPF is designed to provide data about the characteristics, workloads, and opinions of faculty at institutions of higher education in all fifty states. The NSOPF studies are based on nationally representative samples of full- and part-time faculty and instructional staff at public and private not-for-profit two- and four-year degree granting institutions in the United States (Heuer and others, 2005). The NSOPF was selected for this study because it is readily available, contains survey questions of interest, and has been used by numerous other studies to investigate faculty salary equity (Fairweather, 1993; Toutkoushian, 1998; Perna, 2001; Toutkoushian and Conley, 2005; Umbach, 2007, 2009; Porter, Toutkoushian, and Moore, 2008). Furthermore, use of a common data set allows replication of the study by others.

Filters were placed on the 2004 NSOPF to obtain samples that allowed the researcher to assess faculty pay equity by gender among similarly situated faculty. The sample for this study contained all full-time faculty, from doctoral, master's, baccalaureate, and associates institutions with rank and tenure systems whose principal activity was teaching or research. Faculty members who reported salaries at or below $12,500 were not included in the sample. The final sample includes 11,257 faculty members from twenty-six disciplines and 860 institutions. Faculty of the rank professor, associate professor, assistant professor, instructor, and lecturer as well as faculty who were tenured, on the tenure track, and not on the tenure track are included in that sample.

The average base salary for all faculty members included in this study is $63,903. The average base salary for female faculty members ($56,086) is lower than the average base faculty salary for male faculty members ($68,891). Without accounting for any other factors or parsing out institutional and disciplinary differences, there is a $12,805 salary gap between males and females, or approximately 17.0% based on the difference in mean natural log salaries. The descriptive statistics of variables included in this study and a brief description of how they were coded for use with the cross-classified random effects models is provided in Table 5.1.

Results

The first step in building cross-classified random effects models is to determine what amount of variance can be attributed to individual effects, institutional effects, and disciplinary effects; this partitioning of variance is created by running a model without any variables in it and is often referred to as the unconditional model. The results of the unconditional model are shown in Table 5.2. Part A of the table includes the model intercept, which is the predicted natural logged salary for all faculty members in the model when no other variables are accounted for. The second part of the table, Variance Components, includes the random effects results. The coefficients and standard errors are presented in four decimal places, rather than the typical two, as a result of the natural log metric. The random effects values show the partitioning of the variance between individual characteristics, institutional effects and disciplinary effects. Part B shows that approximately 70.5 percent of the variance in faculty salaries can be explained by individual characteristics once disciplinary and institutional effects have been partitioned out. Although individual characteristics explain the majority of base faculty salary, institutional and disciplinary affiliation also play an important role. Institutional affiliation explains approximately 18.2 percent of the variance in faculty salary while disciplinary affiliation explains approximately 11.3 percent of the variance. These results suggest that cross-classified random effects modeling is an appropriate method for examining faculty salary in this study.

NEW DIRECTIONS FOR INSTITUTIONAL RESEARCH • DOI: 10.1002/ir

Table 5.1. Descriptive Statistics, Coding and Centering of Variables in the CCREMs

Variables	Mean	SD	Minimum	Maximum	Codes/Definition
Base Salary	63,903.19	29,193.57	12,760	250,000	Dependent variable
Natural log of salary	10.9785	0.40983	9.45	12.43	
Gender	-0.22	0.98	-1	1	-1 = male, 1 = female
Principal Activity	0.65	0.76	-1	1	-1 = research, 1 = teaching
Gender x Principal Activity	-0.07	1.00	-1	1	
Married/Partnered	0.56	0.83	-1	1	-1 = other, 1 = married/partnered
Dependent Children	0.02	1.00	-1	1	-1 = no dep. children, 1 = dep. children
Minority	-0.59	0.81	-1	1	-1 = white; 1 = minority
Total Publications	0	1	-0.64	9.49	Continuous, z-scored
Classes Taught	0	1	-1.46	17.72	Continuous, z-scored
Unpd. Work within Inst.	0	1	-0.84	5.54	Continuous, z-scored
Unpd. Work outside Inst.	0	1	-0.57	6.55	Continuous, z-scored
Percent Time Instruct	-0.01	1	-2.64	1.4	Continuous, z-scored
Funded Research	-0.28	0.96	-1	1	-1 = not funded, 1 = funded scholarly work
Age	0	1	-2.67	3.38	Continuous, z-scored
Seniority	0	1	-1.08	4.29	Yrs held current job. Continuous, z-scored
Experience	0	1	-1.37	3.53	Yrs since first job in Higher Ed. Cont., z-scored
Doctoral Degree	-0.70	0.46	-1	0	-1 = doctoral degree, 0 = other
Professional Degree	-0.66	0.55	-1	1	-1 = doctoral degree, 1 = prof. degree; 0 = other
Other Degree	-0.43	0.88	-1	1	-1 = doctoral degree; 1 = other degree; 0 = other
Tenured	0.27	0.87	-1	1	-1 = tenure track; 1 = tenured, 0 = other
Tenure Track	-0.28	0.45	-1	0	-1 = tenure track, 0 = other
Not on Tenure Track	-0.11	0.67	-1	1	-1 = tenure track; 1 = not on track, 0 = other
Professor	0.01	0.77	-1	1	-1 = assist. prof.; 1 = prof., 0 = other
Associate Professor	-0.04	0.74	-1	1	-1 = assist. prof.; 1 = associate prof., 0 = other
Assistant Professor	-0.29	0.46	-1	0	-1 = assist. prof., 0 = other
Instructor/lecturer	-0.14	0.65	-1	1	-1 = assist. prof.; 1 = instructor/lecturer, 0 = other

Table 5.1. Continued

Variables	Mean	SD	Minimum	Maximum	Codes/Definition
Institutional Characteristics					
Percent Female	0	1	−1.76	2.55	Aggregated and z-scored
Doctoral	0.12	0.71	−1	1	−1 = masters; 1 = doctoral; 0 = other
Masters	−0.2	0.4	−1	0	−1 = masters; 0 = other
Baccalaureate	−0.04	0.6	−1	1	−1 = masters; 1 = baccalaureate; 0 = other
Associates	0.11	0.71	−1	1	−1 = masters; 1 = associates; 0 = other
Average Faculty Publications	0	1	−1.02	10.77	Aggregated and z-scored
Average Faculty Class Load	0	1	−2.16	11.57	Aggregated and z-scored
Proportion Funded Research	0	1	−1.08	2.99	Aggregated and z-scored
Disciplinary Characteristics					
Percent Female	0	1	−1.71	2.91	Aggregated and z-scored
Social Sciences	−0.23	0.43	−1	0	−1 = social sci.; 0 = other
Professional	−0.08	0.63	−1	1	−1 = social sci.; 1 = prof.; 0 = other
STEM	−0.04	0.66	−1	1	−1 = social sci.; 1 = STEM; 0 = other
Arts & Humanities	−0.04	0.66	−1	1	−1 = social sci.; 1 = arts and humanities; 0 = other
Health Sciences	−0.12	0.59	−1	1	−1 = social sci.; 1 = health sciences; 0 = other
Other Fields	−0.12	0.59	−1	1	−1 = social sci.; 1 = other fields; 0 = other
Average Faculty Publications	0	1	−1.47	2.06	Aggregated and z-scored
Average Faculty Class Load	0	1	−1.67	2.96	Aggregated and z-scored
Proportion Funded Research	0	1	−1.19	2.16	Aggregated and z-scored

Table 5.2. Intercept and Variance Components of the Natural Log of Base Faculty Salary

(a) Fixed Effects	Unconditional Model		
Predictor	b	Sig.	SE
Intercept	10.9433	***	0.0276

(b) Variance components			
Parameter	Estimate		
Variance between institutions	0.0295	***	
Between institutions explained	0.1817		
Variance between disciplines	0.0184	***	
Between disciplines explained	0.1132		
Variance between cells	0.1145		
Between cells explained	0.7051		
Model df	4		
Deviance	8718.55		

Note: ***p < .001, **p < .01, *p < .05

The second step in building cross-classified research models is to add a variety of theoretically derived variables related to the research topic being explored. This study uses a cross-classified random effects model aimed at estimating the faculty gender wage gap once demographic, human capital, and structural factors are taken into account. The level-one or within-cell models in this study are used to describe sources of variation in base salary among faculty from the same institution and discipline. These models are called Female Only, Principal Activity, Demographic, Human Capital, and Rank. Structural characteristics of disciplines and institutions also affect base faculty salary. The level-two, or between-cell, full model is designed to explore how structural effects, such as field and institution type influence base faculty salary. The full model is called the structural model. First, the relationships among the faculty-level characteristics are examined through the within-cell models. Second, the effects of disciplinary and institutional level factors are taken into account in the between-cell model.

Table 5.3 depicts the results of the within-cell models included in this study. The outcome variable is the natural log of base faculty salary. Fixed effects and tests of statistical significance are included in Part A of the table and the variance components are provided in Part B. The coefficients and standard errors are presented in this table with four decimal places as a result of the natural log metric. The Female Only model provides the estimated effect of gender on base faculty salary without controlling for any other factors. In this model, female faculty members earn approximately 14.3 percent less than male faculty members. This percentage gap was calculated by multiplying the gender coefficient by 2 because the

Table 5.3. Level-One Model: Individual Faculty Characteristics

(a) Fixed Effects Predictor	Model 1 Female Only			Model 2 Principal Activity			Model 3 Demographic			Model 4 Human Capital			Model 5 Rank		
	b	Sig.	SE	b	Sig.	SE	b	Sig.	SE	b	Sig.	SE	b	Sig.	SE
Intercept	10.9307	***	0.0261	10.9813	***	0.0254	10.9564	***	0.0254	10.9689	***	0.0216	10.9739	***	0.0209
Gender	-0.0714	***	0.0035	-0.0758	***	0.0047	-0.0726	***	0.0047	-0.02732	***	0.0039	-0.0237	***	0.0038
Principal Activity				-0.0627	***	0.0055	-0.0639	***	0.0055	-0.02426	***	0.0052	-0.0226	***	0.0050
Gender × Principal Activity				0.0088		0.0046	0.0093	*	0.0046	0.00855	*	0.0038	0.0091	*	0.0037
Married/Partnered							0.0256	***	0.0041	0.00588		0.0034	0.0049		0.0033
Dependent Children							-0.0077	*	0.0034	0.00896	**	0.0028	0.0074	**	0.0028
Minority							-0.0230	***	0.0042	-0.00129		0.0034	0.0012		0.0034
Total Publications										0.05609	***	0.0032	0.0421	***	0.0032
Classes Taught										-0.01949	***	0.0032	-0.0170	***	0.0031
Unpd. Work within Inst.										-0.00576	*	0.0027	-0.0051		0.0027
Unpd. Work outside Inst.										0.00448		0.0027	0.0035		0.0026
Percent Instruct										-0.04533	***	0.0037	-0.0404	***	0.0037
Funded										0.02524	***	0.0032	0.0229	***	0.0031
Age										0.02254	***	0.0045	0.0167	***	0.0044
Seniority										0.02602	***	0.0049	0.0171	**	0.0048
Experience										0.05246	***	0.0056	0.0326	***	0.0056
Professional Degree										0.10949	***	0.0119	0.0973	***	0.0116
Other Degree										-0.10145	***	0.0075	-0.0745	***	0.0075
Tenured										0.11433	***	0.0048	0.0576	***	0.0060

	Estimate		Estimate		Estimate		Estimate		Estimate	
Not on Tenure Track							−0.11807	***	0.0052	
									−0.0792	*** 0.0057
Professor									0.1578	*** 0.0068
Associate Professor									0.0232	*** 0.0054
Instructor/ Lecturer									−0.1269	*** 0.0081

(b) Variance Components

Parameter	Estimate		Estimate		Estimate		Estimate		Estimate	
Variance between institutions	0.0292	***	0.0245	***	0.0242	***	0.01559	***	0.01662	***
Between institutions explained	0.1875		0.1640		0.1637		0.1588		0.1755	
Variance between disciplines	0.0162	***	0.0150	***	0.0148	***	0.01009	***	0.0093	***
Between disciplines explained	0.1040		0.1004		0.1002		0.1028		0.0982	
Variance between cells	0.1104		0.1097		0.1090		0.07248		0.06879	
Between cells explained	0.7084		0.7356		0.7361		0.7384		0.7263	
Model df	5		7		10		23		26	
Deviance	8316.49		8152.36		8077.70		3469.40		2941.77	

gender variable used in these models was effect-coded (males = −1, females = 1) rather than dummy-coded. The result was then transformed from a decimal to a percentage.

The estimated gender gap increases to 15.2 percent when principal activity and an interaction effect between gender and principal activity is added in Model 2 (Principal Activity) and decreases slightly to 14.5 percent once demographic factors are included in Model 3 (Demographic). Once human capital characteristics are taken into account in Model 4 (Human Capital), however, the gender gap is substantially reduced to about 5.5 percent. The final within-cell model (Rank), which contrasts differences in rank, shows that females earned approximately 4.7 percent less than their male counterparts once all other within-cell factors were taken into account. This equates to a $2,765 salary gap between male and female faculty members.

The results of the complete within-cell model (Rank) show that Principal Activity (teaching or research) was a significant and negative predictor of salary. Faculty whose principal activity was teaching earned approximately 4.5 percent less, or about $2,633, than faculty whose principal activity was research. There was also a significant interaction effect between gender and principal activity, indicating that there is a significant difference in salaries between male faculty whose principal activity is research, female faculty whose principal activity is research, male faculty whose principal activity is teaching, and male faculty whose principal activity is teaching. To describe the effect of the gender–principal activity interaction, the model intercept, coefficients for gender, principal activity, and interaction effect between gender and principal activity were used to obtain the predicted salary for male and female faculty whose principal activity was either teaching or research. The formulas used can be represented as

y' = Intercept + Male + Teaching − Gender and Principal Activity
    Interaction

y' = Intercept + Female + Teaching + Gender and Principal Activity
    Interaction

y' = Intercept + Male + Research − Gender and Principal Activity
    Interaction

y' = Intercept + Female + Research + Gender and Principal Activity
    Interaction

Figure 5.1 depicts the interaction effect between gender and principal activity on the natural log of base faculty salary for the final within-cell

Figure 5.1. Alternative Depictions of the Interaction Effect between Gender and Principal Activity on the Natural Log of Salary, Rank Model

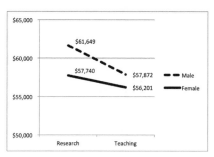

Panel (a): Salary gaps by gender

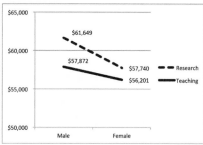

Panel (b): Salary gaps by principal activity

model (Rank). The figure illustrates that regardless of principal activity, male faculty have higher average salaries than female faculty even after demographic, human capital, and rank are taken into account. The figure also illustrates that the salary gap is larger between male and female faculty focusing on research than it is for male and female faculty focusing on teaching. Alternatively, the difference in earnings between teaching and research is larger for male faculty than female faculty.

After accounting for within-cell faculty characteristics, the gender salary gap can be examined in context with structural, disciplinary and institutional factors. Table 5.4 shows the results of the full cross-classified model. The first part of the table shows the fixed effects and tests of statistical significance, and the second part of the table provides the random effects. The coefficients and standard errors are presented in this table with four decimal places as a result of the natural log metric. The Structural model is designed to examine the effect of institution and discipline type on base faculty salary and determine whether there are significant overall differences in salary between male and female faculty.

The Structural model shows that after all the other factors in the model are taken into account, the overall gender gap was reduced to 4.8 percent. The model also shows that institutional affiliation has a significant effect on base faculty salary. After accounting for principal activity, demographic, and human capital characteristics, faculty members in doctoral universities are predicted to earn approximately $61,934. Faculty in master's ($56,690), baccalaureate ($53,877), and associates institutions ($59,192) all have lower average salaries than doctoral institutions, although faculty in associates colleges have the second highest average salaries of the four institution types.

The Structural model also shows that disciplinary affiliation affects base faculty salary. Professional fields, Arts and Humanities, and Health

Table 5.4. Level-Two Model: Structural Characteristics

(a) Fixed Effects Predictor	Structural				(b) Variance Components Parameter	
	b	Sig.	SE	P-value		
Intercept	10.9655	***	0.0153	0.000	Variance between institutions	0.0145***
Institutional Characteristics					Between institutions explained	0.1668
Percent female					Variance between disciplines	0.0037***
Doctoral	0.0683	***	0.0088	0.000	Between disciplines explained	0.0430
Bachelors	−0.0711	***	0.0111	0.000	Variance between cells	0.0687
Associates	0.0230	*	0.0104	0.027	Between cells explained	0.7902
Disciplinary Characteristics					Estimated parameters	34
Percent female					Deviance	2837.18
Professional	0.0726	*	0.0289	0.012		
STEM fields	0.0024		0.0261	0.927		
Fine Arts & Humanities	−0.1150	***	0.0262	0.000		
Health Sciences	0.1116	**	0.0325	0.001		
Other Fields	−0.0297		0.0324	0.360		
Individual Characteristics						
Gender	−0.0241	***	0.0038	0.000		
Principal Activity	−0.0199	***	0.0050	0.000		
Female × Primary Activity	0.0092	*	0.0037	0.013		
Married/Partnered	0.0048		0.0033	0.138		
Dependent Children	0.0075	**	0.0028	0.007		
Minority	0.0015		0.0034	0.661		
Career Publications	0.0404	***	0.0032	0.000		
Classes Taught	−0.0157	***	0.0031	0.000		
Unpd. Work within Inst.	−0.0043		0.0027	0.104		
Unpd. Work outside Inst.	0.0036		0.0026	0.174		
Percent Instruct	−0.0388	***	0.0037	0.000		
Funded	0.0224	***	0.0031	0.000		
Age	0.0165	***	0.0044	0.000		
Seniority	0.0167	**	0.0048	0.001		
Experience	0.0329	***	0.0056	0.000		
Professional Degree	0.0979	***	0.0115	0.000		
Other Degree	−0.0742	***	0.0075	0.000		
Tenured	0.0577	***	0.0060	0.000		
Not on Tenure Track	−0.0801	***	0.0059	0.000		
Professor	0.1597	***	0.0068	0.000		
Associate Professor	0.0239	***	0.0055	0.000		
Instructor/Lecturer	−0.1301	***	0.0081	0.000		

Note: ***$p < .001$, **$p < .01$, *$p < .05$

Sciences all have significant effects on salary as compared with the Social Sciences. The predicted average salaries for faculty working in the discipline types included in this study are: Arts and Humanities ($51,564), Social Sciences ($55,465), Other Fields ($56,156), STEM Fields ($57,986), Professional ($62,200), and Health Sciences ($64,679).

There was a significant interaction effect between gender and principal activity (teaching or research) in the Structural model. The effect of this interaction is depicted in Figure 5.2. In this figure, the gap between males and females is larger for faculty whose principal activity is research (6.4 percent) than for faculty whose principal activity is teaching (2.9 percent). The figure shows that there is a more pronounced difference in salary between male faculty members whose principal activity is either teaching or research than it is for female faculty. Finally, male faculty members have higher average salaries than female faculty in both research- and teaching-oriented positions, even after demographic, human capital, and structural factors are taken into account.

Conclusion

This study, which applied cross-classified random effects modeling, shows that pay differentials continue to exist and remain a troublesome challenge for higher education. This study shows that even after controlling for institutional and disciplinary characteristics, principal activity, human capital, and demographic factors, female faculty members earn less than male faculty members. Although this study cannot account for all of the variation in faculty salary, these results suggest a possible systematic underpayment of female faculty in higher education.

This study provides essential statistical information about faculty salary equity in higher education on a national scale. It shows that the

Figure 5.2. Alternative Depictions of the Interaction Effect between Gender and Principal Activity on the Natural Log of Salary, Structural Model

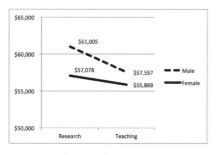

Panel (a): Salary gaps by gender

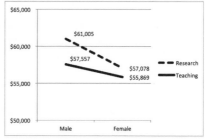

Panel (b): Salary gaps by principal activity

NEW DIRECTIONS FOR INSTITUTIONAL RESEARCH • DOI: 10.1002/ir

gender salary gap continues to persist in higher education. Use of large-scale data sets and techniques such as cross-classified random effects modeling can help inform administrators about macro-level issues and trends and inform how they may benefit from reexamining their policies, including how salary structures inform the degree to which teaching- and research-oriented work is valued.

References

American Association of University Professors. "Faculty Salary and Faculty Distribution Fact Sheet 2003–2004." Retrieved October 5, 2011, from http://www.aaup.org/AAUP/pubsres/research/2003–04factsheet.htm.

Barbezat, D. "Affirmative Action in Higher Education: Have Two Decades Altered Salary Differentials by Sex and Race?" *Research in Labor Economics,* 1989, *10,* 107–156.

Barbezat, D. "Updating Estimates of Male-Female Salary Differentials in the Academic Labor Market." *Economics Letters,* 1991, 36(2), 191–195.

Barbezat, D. A., and Hughes, J. W. "Salary Structure Effects and the Gender Gap in Academia." *Research in Higher Education,* 2005, *46*(6), 621–639.

Becker, W. E., and Toutkoushian, R. K. "Measuring Gender Bias in the Salaries of Tenured Faculty Members." In R. K. Toutkoushian (ed.), *Unresolved Issues in Conducting Salary Equity Studies.* New Directions for Institutional Research, no. 117. San Francisco: Jossey-Bass, 2003.

Bellas, M. L. "Faculty Salaries: Still a Cost of Being Female?" *Social Science Quarterly,* 1993, 74(1), 62–75.

Beretvas, S. N. "Cross-Classified Random Effects Models." In A. Connell and D. McCoach (eds.), *Multilevel Modeling of Educational Data.* Charlotte, N.C.: Information Age Publishing, 2008.

England, P. "The Failure of Human Capital Theory to Explain Occupational Sex Segregation." *Journal of Human Resources,* 1982, 17(3), 358–370.

Fairweather, J. S. "Faculty Reward Structures: Toward Institutional and Professional Homogenization." *Research in Higher Education,* 1993, *34*(5), 603–623.

Heuer, R., and others. 2004 National Study of Postsecondary Faculty (nsopf:04) Methodology Report (NCES 2006-179). Washington, DC: National Center for Education Statistics, 2005.

Perna, L. W. "Sex Differences in Faculty Salaries: A Cohort Analysis." *Review of Higher Education,* 2001, *24*(3), 283–307.

Perna L. W. "The Status of Women and Minorities among Community College Faculty." *Research in Higher Education,* 2003, *44*(2), 205–240.

Porter, S. R., Toutkoushian, R. K., and Moore J. V. "Pay Inequities for Recently Hired Faculty, 1988–2004." *Review of Higher Education,* 2008, *31*(4), 465–487.

Raudenbush, S. W., and Bryk, A. S. *Hierarchical Linear Models: Applications and Data Analysis Methods.* (2nd ed.). Thousand Oaks, Calif.: Sage Publications, 2002.

Raudenbush, S., and others. *Hierarchical Linear and Nonlinear Modeling.* Lincolnwood, Ill.: Scientific Software International, 2004.

Smart, J. "Gender Equity in Academic Rank and Salary." *Review of Higher Education,* 1991, *14*(4), 511–526.

Tolbert, P. S. "Organizations and Inequality: Sources of Earnings Differences between Male and Female Faculty." *Sociology of Education,* 1986, 59, 227–235.

Toutkoushian, R. K. "Racial and Marital Status Differences in Faculty Pay." *Journal of Higher Education,* 1998, 69(5), 513–541.

Toutkoushian, R., and Conley, V. "Progress for Women in Academe, yet Inequities Persist. Evidence from NSOPF: 99." *Research in Higher Education,* 2005, *46*(1), 1–28.

Umbach, P. D. "Gender Equity in the Academic Labor Market: An Analysis of Academic Disciplines." *Research in Higher Education,* 2007, *48*(2), 169–192.

Umbach, P. D. "Sex Segregation in Academic Labor Markets and Equity in Faculty Pay." Paper presented at the 34th Annual Conference of the Association for the Study of Higher Education, Vancouver, B.C., November 5–7, 2009.

Welch, F. "The Human Capital Theory: Education, Discrimination, and Life Cycles." *American Economic Review,* 1975, *65*(2) 63–73.

LAURA E. MEYERS recently graduated from the University of Washington with a Ph.D. in educational leadership and policy studies.

6

This chapter describes an institutional study of the effects of a learning community on student learning by utilizing multilevel modeling.

Multilevel Modeling: Applications to Research on the Assessment of Student Learning, Engagement, and Developmental Outcomes

Pu-Shih Daniel Chen, Kristina Cragg

Multilevel modeling began to emerge in research literature in the 1960s and 1970s. As reported by Raudenbush and Bryk (2002), multilevel modeling is known by different names in various disciplines: in biometric research, it is referred to as mixed-effects models or random-effects models (Blood, Cabral, Heeren, and Cheng, 2010; Schall, 1991); in economics, it is referred to as random-coefficient regression models (Moulton, 1986); and in statistics, it is often referred to as covariance components models. Although the term *multilevel modeling* may be less familiar to institutional research (IR) professionals, most are probably familiar with the term *hierarchical linear modeling* (HLM). Regardless of what the method is called, all of these methods refer to a statistical modeling strategy in which the parameters of a regression model are given a probability model and therefore have their own parameters (Gelman and Hill, 2007). Many modern statistics programs, including HLM, R, SAS, SPSS, STATA, and MLwiN, can be utilized to construct and analyze multilevel models. IR professionals who wish to conduct multilevel modeling can choose from an array of statistics programs. There are also many books available on the topic of multilevel modeling (for example, see Kreft and de Leeuw, 1998; Snijders and Bosker, 1999; Hox, 2002; Goldstein, 2003; Luke, 2004;

NEW DIRECTIONS FOR INSTITUTIONAL RESEARCH, no. 154, Summer 2012 © Wiley Periodicals, Inc.
Published online in Wiley Online Library (wileyonlinelibrary.com) • DOI: 10.1002/ir.20016

Bickel, 2007; Gelman and Hill, 2007). See http://tinyurl.com/3ywf8ap for an overview of many statistical programs that can do multilevel modeling and http://tinyurl.com/25caexj for multilevel modeling books.

Even as multilevel modeling gains popularity among academic researchers, it is still underutilized in the field of institutional research. The hesitation to conduct multilevel modeling analysis by IR professionals is caused largely by a lack of understanding. Many hold the view that multilevel modeling is for academic research and not appropriate for institutional research. Some IR professionals question the relevance and utility of applying multilevel modeling to higher education settings. Many also believe that multilevel modeling is very difficult to learn and master. Additionally, because of the general unfamiliarity with multilevel modeling in the institutional research profession, many IR professionals lack understanding of how to present results in a way that can be understood by laypersons.

In the book *Applications of Intermediate/Advanced Statistics in Institutional Research*, Porter (2005) pointed out that higher education institutions by their nature are multilevel structures. Campus divisions, colleges, departments, academic programs, and classes are all nested in a hierarchical structure. Likewise, college student life can also be examined as a multilevel configuration in which individuals are nested in classes, residence halls, learning communities, student organizations, and the campus. Student learning does not happen in isolation but in a nested and intercorrelated environment. Thus, multilevel modeling can be a powerful and appropriate tool to study institutional practices and their impacts on students and faculty.

Purpose of Study and Research Questions

Understanding the suitability of multilevel modeling in the context of institutional research may ease the doubts of some IR professionals. However, the need for training on how to conduct and report multilevel modeling analysis remains. A major roadblock hindering the proliferation of multilevel modeling in institutional research is the perception that multilevel modeling is difficult to learn and that the sample size requirement is very rigid. Many IR professionals seem to think that multilevel modeling can be applied only to cross-institutional studies, as intramural analysis does not provide a large enough sample size within each level. This observation is partially correct, but with a carefully designed data collection strategy, many intramural studies can be analyzed using multilevel modeling.

This chapter provides an example of one typical institutional study that utilizes multilevel modeling to examine student learning outcomes. Using data from a four-year university located in the southeastern United States, a study of the effects of learning communities on student learning was conducted. Discussion of results of the study is followed by examples of effective strategies for reporting multilevel modeling results to institutional stakeholders and decision makers. Three research questions guided this study:

1. Does high school academic performance affect first-year college students' likelihood to participate in learning communities?
2. Does participating in learning communities affect first-year students' academic persistence?
3. Do the types and characteristics of the learning communities have a differential effect on first-year students' GPAs?

Literature Review

As colleges and universities seek to be more efficient with existing resources while improving retention and graduation rates, more and more institutions choose to utilize learning communities as a way of promoting student success. Many higher education administrators believe that learning communities will reduce unused seat spaces and increase student retention rates. This section provides background on the history and current research pertaining to the learning community and a discussion of its impact on student learning.

Historical Beginnings of Learning Communities. Influenced by John Dewey's focus on student-centered learning, philosopher and education theorist Alexander Meiklejohn helped the University of Wisconsin establish the Experimental College in 1927 to provide an interdisciplinary undergraduate curriculum focusing on democracy. Meiklejohn's experimental project has been recognized by many as the first learning community (Smith, 2001; Tinto, 2003). Unfortunately, the Experimental College at the University of Wisconsin was short-lived. After it was discontinued in 1932, the idea of the learning community went dormant for several decades until Joseph Tussman, one of Meiklejohn's students, established the learning community program at the University of California at Berkeley in 1969 (Smith, 2001). Similar to the learning community established by his predecessor, Tussman's program was short-lived. Although both Meiklejohn's and Tussman's early models were limited in the students they served and the scope of influence on student learning (Halpin, 1990), these early models of learning communities evolved over time into more mature and comprehensive programs that would flourish in the late twentieth and early twenty-first centuries (Smith, MacGregor, Matthews, and Gabelnick, 2004).

Elements of Learning Communities. Tinto (1999) cited five conditions necessary for undergraduate student success: (1) high and clear expectations, (2) support, (3) feedback, (4) involvement, and (5) relevant learning. Although the first three conditions occur in many first-year classes and student support services, the latter two tend to happen less frequently in the lower divisions of undergraduate coursework. Learning communities offer a means to provide these two conditions to lower-division undergraduates if they are designed and integrated with other first-year courses.

The structure of learning communities varies from institution to institution, but the common premise is that learning communities bring together students and faculty through a common purpose or vision in two or more courses. One common subset of learning communities is the Freshman Learning Community, which focuses on enriching and improving the overall experience of first-year college students (Soldner, Lee, and Duby, 1999). Students typically participate in learning communities based on academic majors, interests, residence halls, hobbies, cultures, religious affiliations, and intramural sports.

Most learning communities in American colleges and universities today build on Tinto's Model of Interaction to provide a theoretical foundation for research about student success (Halpin, 1990). Learning communities provide an atmosphere that encourages student participation and motivates students with peer-involved learning. In some cases, institutions may restructure curricula to strengthen connections between students and faculty. Examples of such curriculum changes include implementation of seminars or peer-advising components, such as student-organized study sessions designed to help students link their academic work with active and increased interaction with peers and faculty. Learning communities may also increase coherence among students and create a sense of common purpose and community (Kellogg, 1999).

Impact of Learning Communities on Students. Students who participate in learning communities have been found to have higher graduation rates and report a more enriched college experience (Shapiro and Levine, 1999; Hurd and Stein, 2004; Laufgraben and Shapiro, 2004; Smith, MacGregor, Matthews, and Gabelnick, 2004; Pascarella and Terenzini, 2005). Additionally, students in learning communities report an increased sense of responsibility to participate in the learning experience and an increased awareness of their responsibility for their learning and the learning of others (Laufgraben and Shapiro, 2004; Smith, MacGregor, Matthews, and Gabelnick, 2004). This increased awareness of the student role in learning supports the conclusion that learning communities are positively linked to engagement as well as to student self-reported learning outcomes and overall satisfaction with the institution (Zhao and Kuh, 2004).

Impact of Learning Communities on Institutions. Advantages of learning communities extend beyond the success of students; they positively influence the institution as well. Learning communities benefit the institution by providing a means to serve a growing diverse student population while centralizing elements that improve the overall campus climate and reinforce positive views of the institution (Tinto, 1999; Hurd and

Stein, 2004; Laufgraben and Shapiro, 2004; Smith, MacGregor, Matthews, and Gabelnick, 2004). A stronger connection to the institution through faculty, staff, and students creates an increased probability for student retention (Terenzini and Pascarella, 1980; Tinto, 2003; Braxton, Hirschy, and McClendon, 2004). Learning communities also allow institutions to plan for sufficient—not too many or too few—seats in freshmen courses as the courses are purposefully scheduled.

Methods

The following paragraphs describe the methodological approach for this study.

Population and Sample. The population of this study is first-year students enrolled at a four-year university located in the southeastern United States. The Carnegie Foundation for the Advancement of Teaching classifies the university as a large master's college and university (Master's I) with a total enrollment of approximately 13,000. For the purpose of this study, we utilized a sample of data from the fall 2009 first-year cohort including 2,595 students. Of the 2,595 students, 799 (30.8 percent) participated in the university's learning community program. Each learning community has approximately twenty-five students enrolling together in a first-year seminar, an English course, and a social science course. The demographic characteristics of the sample can be found in Table 6.1.

Data Collection. Data for the study were extracted from panels in the university student information system database, including admissions, financial aid, and academics. These data were merged and cleaned prior to analysis.

Variables and Data Analysis. The first research question—Does high school academic performance affect first-year college students' likelihood to participate in learning communities?—was answered with a logistic regression analysis. Logistic regression allows researchers to predict a discrete outcome from a set of independent variables that may be continuous, discrete, dichotomous, or a mix of variables (Tabachnick and Fidell, 2007). For the first research question, the dependent variable is participation in a learning community (1 = yes; 0 = no); and the independent variables are high school grade point average (GPA), student's gender (male = 1; female = 0), race/ethnicity (White/Caucasian was used as the baseline comparison group), enrollment status (full-time = 0; part-time = 1), living arrangement (off-campus = 0; on-campus = 1), and financial aid status (students who received no financial aid were used as the baseline comparison group).

A logistic regression analysis was also used to answer the second research question—Does participating in learning communities affect first-year students' academic persistence? The dependent variable for the

Table 6.1. Demographic Characteristics of the Sample

	First-Year Cohort (2009)	Learning Community Participants	Non-Learning Community Students
Number of students	2595	799	1796
Average high school GPA	3.07	3.03	3.09
Gender			
Male	38.7%	33.4%	41.0%
Female	61.3%	66.6%	59.0%
Race/Ethnicity			
White/Caucasian	51.7%	47.4%	53.6%
African American	41.3%	47.1%	38.7%
Hispanic	2.3%	1.9%	2.5%
Asian	0.8%	0.4%	1.0%
Native American	0.4%	0.5%	0.4%
Other	3.3%	2.7%	3.7%
Enrollment status			
Full-time	96.1%	98.5%	95.0%
Part-time	3.9%	1.5%	5.0%
Living arrangement			
On-campus	74.1%	85.1%	69.2%
Off-campus	25.9%	14.9%	30.8%
Financial aid status			
State-funded scholarship	54.1%	53.3%	54.5%
Grants[1]	46.4%	46.7%	46.3%
Loan	63.4%	67.1%	61.7%
No aid	11.5%	11.0%	11.7%
Others	55.7%	55.7%	55.7%
Academic disciplines			
Arts and Sciences	53.4%	52.2%	53.9%
Fine Arts/Music	9.6%	4.9%	11.6%
Business	9.6%	6.5%	10.9%
Education	17.4%	18.2%	17.1%
Nursing	10.0%	18.1%	6.5%
Retained to 2nd year			
Yes	88.0%	93.1%	85.7%
No	12.0%	6.9%	14.3%

[1] Most students in this category received federal grants, but a few also received state grants.

second research question is the first-year student's academic persistence to the second year (retained to second year = 1; drop before second year = 0). The independent variables include participation in a learning community (yes = 1; no = 0), high school GPA, student gender (male = 1; female = 0), race/ethnicity (White/Caucasian was used as the baseline comparison group), enrollment status (full-time = 0; part-time = 1), living arrangement (off-campus = 0; on-campus = 1), and financial aid status (students who received no financial aid were used as the baseline comparison group).

NEW DIRECTIONS FOR INSTITUTIONAL RESEARCH • DOI: 10.1002/ir

The third research question—Do the types and characteristics of the learning communities have a differential effect on first-year students' GPA?—was answered with an HLM analysis (Raudenbush and Bryk, 2002). The assumption underlying HLM analysis is that the types and characteristics of learning communities may have a differential impact on first-year students' GPA. By using HLM, we can partition the variance attributable to the individual and the variance attributable to the learning communities. The dependent variable for the HLM analysis is the first-year students' GPA. The individual (level-one) independent variables for the initial model include high school GPA, student gender (male = 1; female = 0), race/ethnicity (White/Caucasian was used as the baseline comparison group), enrollment status (full-time = 0; part-time = 1), living arrangement (off-campus = 0; on-campus = 1), and financial aid status (students who received no financial aid were used as the baseline comparison group). The level-two independent variables for the initial model are types of learning community (theme-based or discipline-based), size of the learning community, percentage of students who receive grants, and percentage of students who live on campus. Analysis involved the use of a one-way analysis of variance (ANOVA) model, a means-as-outcomes model, and a random coefficients regression model for each level-one and level-two independent variable prior to determining that an intercepts-as-outcomes model would be fit best. The modeling results are presented in the next section.

Results

The following paragraphs provide the results for the research questions that guided this study.

Research Question 1. The first research question asks if a first-year college student's high school academic performance affects his or her likelihood to join a learning community. The results show that students with a higher high school GPA are less likely to join a learning community than students with a lower high school GPA (odds ratio = .61, $p = .001$; Table 6.2). Other factors that may affect a first-year student's likelihood to participate in learning communities include gender (male < female, odds ratio = .69, $p < .001$), enrollment status (part-time < full-time, odds ratio = .1, $p = .02$), and living arrangement (on-campus > off-campus, odds ratio = 2.17, $p < .001$). Generally speaking, the results of the study are in agreement with the literature that indicated that female, full-time, and residence hall students engaged more in educationally meaningful activities than male, part-time, and commuting students (Pike, 2004; Zhao and Kuh, 2004; Kinzie and others, 2007). Findings also indicate that race, ethnicity, and financial aid status do not have a statistically significant impact on first-year students' likelihood to join a learning community.

New Directions for Institutional Research • DOI: 10.1002/ir

Table 6.2. Logistic Regression Results for Research Question 1

Predictor	β	SE of β	p Value	e^{β} (Odds Ratio)
Constant	.14	.43		
High School GPA	−0.49	0.15	.001	0.61
Gender (1 = male, 0 = female)	−0.38	0.09	<.001	0.69
Race/Ethnicity (African American)[1]	0.16	0.11	.12	1.18
Race/Ethnicity (Hispanic)[1]	−0.52	0.26	.05	0.60
Race/Ethnicity (Asian)[1]	−0.68	0.65	.29	0.50
Race/Ethnicity (Native American)[1]	−0.97	1.09	.37	0.38
Race/Ethnicity (Other)[1]	0.51	0.88	.57	1.66
Enrollment Status (0 = full-time, 1 = part-time)	−2.32	1.03	.02	0.10
Living Arrangement (0 = off-campus, 1 = on-campus)	0.78	0.12	<.001	2.17
Financial Aids (state-funded scholarship)[2]	0.03	0.24	.89	1.03
Financial Aids (loans)[2]	−0.05	0.10	.63	0.95
Financial Aids (Grants)[2]	−0.09	0.10	.34	0.91
Financial Aids (Others)[2]	0.22	0.23	.34	1.24

[1] White/Caucasian was used as the comparison group.
[2] Students who received no financial aid were used as the comparison group.

Research Question 2. In the second research question, we asked if participating in learning communities affects first-year students' academic persistence. Persistence, for this study, is defined as a student's continuous enrollment at the same institution at the beginning of the second academic year. According to the results of this analysis (see Table 6.3), participating in a learning community does not have a statistically significant impact on first-year students' persistence to the second year (odds ratio = 1.21, p = .26). Of all the student characteristics studied, only being an African American (higher than the baseline group, odds ratio = 1.73, p = .004) or Native American (lower than the baseline group, odds ratio = .19, p = .03) and enrollment status (part-time < full-time, odds ratio =.42, p = .05) have statistically significant impacts on academic persistence. Participation in a learning community, high school GPA, gender, living arrangement, and financial aid status do not have statistically significant impact on first-year students' academic persistence.

Research Question 3. Results from research question 3 were broken into four sections.

HLM One-Way ANOVA Model. To answer the third research question, an HLM was built to investigate the impacts of the types and characteristics of learning communities on first-year students' GPAs. Before estimating the full, two-level HLM to examine the effects of individual

Table 6.3. Logistic Regression Results for Research Question 2

Predictor	β	SE of β	p Value	e^β (Odds Ratio)
Constant	0.83	0.67		
Participation in a Learning Community	0.19	0.17	0.26	1.21
High School GPA	0.27	0.23	0.24	1.32
Gender (1 = male, 0 = female)	0.00	0.15	0.99	1.00
Race/Ethnicity (African American)[1]	0.55	0.19	0.004	1.73
Race/Ethnicity (Hispanic)[1]	0.00	0.35	0.99	1.00
Race/Ethnicity (Asian)[1]	0.64	1.04	0.54	1.91
Race/Ethnicity (Native American)[1]	−1.64	0.75	0.03	0.19
Race/Ethnicity (Other)[1]	0.18	1.13	0.87	1.20
Enrollment Status (0 = full-time, 1 = part-time)	−0.86	0.44	0.05	0.42
Living Arrangement (0 = off-campus, 1 = on-campus)	0.24	0.17	0.17	1.27
Financial Aids (state-funded scholarship)[2]	0.41	0.40	0.30	1.51
Financial Aids (loans)[2]	0.23	0.17	0.17	1.26
Financial Aids (Grants)[2]	0.08	0.17	0.62	1.09
Financial Aids (Others)[2]	−0.04	0.38	0.92	0.96

[1] White/Caucasian was used as the comparison group.
[2] Students who received no financial aid were used as the comparison group.

characteristics and learning communities on student GPAs, we used a one-way ANOVA model, or so-called null model, to estimate the proportion of variance that exists between and within learning communities (Raudenbush and Bryk, 2002). The results show that the proportion of variance between learning communities is 9 percent, indicating that 91 percent of the variance in student GPA can be attributed to individual factors and 9 percent can be attributed to differences among learning communities.

Means-as-Outcomes Model. After estimating the one-way ANOVA model, means-as-outcomes models were constructed to examine which level-two independent variables would have an impact in reducing unexplained variance. At this point, the researcher must make some choices based on the purpose of the study. If the study is to establish a theoretically sound statistical model for the purpose of explaining an educational phenomenon, the variables included in the HLM model must be theoretically based and have good literature support. Most academic research in social sciences falls into this category. However, if the purpose of the study is to improve the predictive power of the statistical model, only independent variables that have statistically significant effects on the outcomes should be included in the HLM model. Many studies conducted by IR professionals fall into the second category. For example, an IR professional

Table 6.4. HLM Results from the Means-as-Outcomes Model

Variables	T	$\Delta\tau$	Keep in Model
Number of participants in each learning community	0.057	0.026	Yes
Percentage of students who received federal or state grants	0.084	<0.001	No
Percentage of students living on campus	0.083	0.001	No
Learning community types	0.082	0.001	No

may want to know what variables predict student retention at a particular institution. The IR professional should start the study by reviewing literature on student retention and finding out what individual and institutional variables have been proved to effect student retention. The IR professional then builds an initial model based on the variables found in the literature. After testing the model, the IR professional may find that some variables do not work for this particular institution as they were stated in the literature, whereas other variables that were disregarded in the literature have great predicting power on student retention at the institution. At this point, the IR professional may choose to include those variables that have statistically significant predictive power in the model instead of variables with literature support. This is the approach we took to build our HLM models for this institutional study.

By inserting each level-two independent variable into the model, the variables that reduced unexplained variance were distinguished from those that did not. Table 6.4 shows the results of the means-as-outcomes model. After reviewing the change in τ—which is unexplained variance in the model—we decided to retain the size of the learning community variable (reduce τ from .08352 to .05731) in the final model. The types of learning community, the percentage of students who received federal or state grants, and the percentage of students living on campus were excluded, as they did not appear to have an impact on the outcomes.

Random-Coefficients Regression Model. After estimating and reviewing the results of the means-as-outcomes models, the modeling exercise continued by estimating the random-coefficients regression model, also known as the level-one model or the individual-level model (Raudenbush and Bryk, 2002). Just as the means-as-outcomes models tested the variance explaining power of level-two variables, the random-coefficients regression model tests and establishes the individual-level independent variables before estimating the full, intercept, and slopes-as-outcomes model. The results of the random-coefficients regression model are shown in Table 6.5. Due to reasons stated in the means-as-outcomes models, we chose to keep state-funded scholarship (reduce σ^2 from .843 to .695) and high school GPA (reduce σ^2 from .843 to .638) in the final model.

Table 6.5. HLM Results from the Random-Coefficients Regression Model

Variables	σ^2	$\Delta\sigma^2$	Keep in Model
State-funded scholarship	0.695	0.148	Yes
Loans	0.817	0.026	No
Grants	0.841	0.002	No
No aid	0.809	0.034	No
Gender	0.820	0.023	No
White/Caucasian	0.831	0.012	No
African American	0.831	0.012	No
Hispanic	0.831	0.013	No
Asian	0.843	0.001	No
American Indian Alaskan Native	0.844	−0.001	No
Native Hawaiian/Pacific Islander	0.844	−0.001	No
Two or more races	0.842	0.001	No
Other race/ethnicity	0.833	0.010	No
Race/ethnicity unknown	0.843	0.001	No
Live on campus	0.806	0.037	No
Full time	0.834	0.010	No
First-time full-time freshmen	0.828	0.015	No
High school GPA	0.638	0.205	Yes

Intercepts-as-Outcomes Model. The fourth and final step of the modeling process is to establish the between-learning-community model by allowing the intercept to vary by learning communities. We then modeled the intercept by level-two independent variables. Here is the final model:

$$Y_{ij} = \beta_{0j} + \beta_{1j}(State\ Scholarship) + \beta_{2j}(Other\ Aid)$$
$$+ \beta_{3j}(High\ School\ GPA) + r_{ij}$$

$$\beta_{0j} = \gamma_{00} + \gamma_{01}(Number\ of\ Participants) + u_{0j}$$

$$\beta_{1j} = \gamma_{10} + u_{1j}$$

$$\beta_{2j} = \gamma_{20} + u_{2j}$$

$$\beta_{3j} = \gamma_{30} + u_{3j}$$

Table 6.6 displays the summary effects of individual- and community-level variables on first-year students' GPA. According to the results, a first-year student's past academic achievement, as measured by high school GPA, plays a very important role in his or her first-year academic performance ($\beta = .831$, $p < .001$). No community-level variable has a statistically significant effect on first-year students' GPA.

Table 6.6. HLM Results from the Intercepts-as-Outcomes Model

	Coefficient	p-Value
Community-Level Variables		
Intercept	.456	
Number of participants in each learning community	−.02	.12
Individual-Level Variables		
State-funded scholarship	.045	.71
Other aid	.238	.03
High school GPA	.85	<.001
Variance Components		
Variance between learning communities	.057	
Variance between explained	31%	
Variance within learning communities	.63	
Variance within explained	25%	

Interpreting and Presenting the Results

Although statistically significant findings are of utmost importance to many academic researchers, many times nonsignificant findings can be equally valuable in promoting effective institutional practices and decision making. The results of this study will be used to demonstrate how to present multilevel analysis results to senior administrators and stakeholders.

This institutional study shows that, at the university studied, first-year students with higher high school GPAs and male, part-time, and commuting students are less likely to join a learning community than their counterparts. The results also indicate that participating in a learning community does not have a statistically significant effect on first-year students' persistence to the second year. The only factor that seems to have an impact on first-year students' GPA is their high school GPA (see Figure 6.1). Interpretation of these results suggests these conclusions:

The learning community program at the university still needs more research to determine its effects on student learning. A qualitative assessment plan will accompany this study and greatly improve understanding of the impact of learning community on student learning at this institution. The university might consider analyzing additional characteristics such as type of group assignments, physical design of the classrooms, and degree of collaboration among faculty within a learning community, and so forth, to examine other components that may influence students' academic persistence at the institution and incorporate those components into the learning communities.

NEW DIRECTIONS FOR INSTITUTIONAL RESEARCH • DOI: 10.1002/ir

Figure 6.1. Factors that Have an Impact on First-Year College Students' GPA

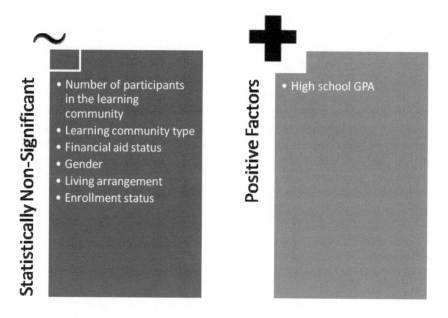

After controlling for other factors, African American students tend to have a higher retention rate than white students. The university could examine which elements promote African American student retention at the institution and replicate these elements to other students.

It is not clear why students with higher high school GPAs are less likely to join learning communities. The university could conduct a qualitative assessment project to examine this issue in more depth. Changes may be required in the structure of the learning communities or in the way learning communities are promoted in order to attract more academically qualified students.

Male, part-time, and commuting students are known to be less engaged than female, full-time, students living on campus. Although this phenomenon is not unique to this university, the faculty and administrators could discuss ways to engage this group of students.

Although they are a small group (fewer than fifty students at the university), Native American students are retained at a much lower rate than other students at this university after controlling for other factors. Literature has shown that Native American students experience unique personal, cultural, and academic challenges on college campuses (Lee, Donlan, and Brown, 2010). The university should take appropriate actions to support and engage this group of students.

Conclusion

In this study, real student data were used to execute an institutional study that examines the effects of learning communities on student learning using multilevel modeling. Because this is a single-institution study, the results may not apply to other institutions. However, the purpose of this study is not to generalize the findings but to demonstrate the utility of multilevel modeling in institutional research for data-driven decision making at a specific campus. As IR professionals are well aware, quantitative assessment has its limitations. For example, institutional culture and campus climate cannot be easily reflected through quantitative studies. IR professionals should utilize multiple tools to assess the effectiveness of institutional policies and practices. Nevertheless, we hope that through this study, IR professionals will become more informed about multilevel modeling and more likely to utilize this powerful tool to improve institutional practices and decision making.

References

Bickel, R. *Multilevel Analysis for Applied Research: It's Just Regression.* New York: Guilford Press, 2007.

Blood, E. A., Cabral, H, Heeren, T., and Cheng, D. M. "Performance of Mixed Effects Models in the Analysis of Mediated Longitudinal Data." *BMC Medical Research Methodology,* 2010, *10,* 16.

Braxton, J. M., Hirschy, A. S., and McClendon, S. A. (2004). "Understanding and Reducing College Student Departure." *ASHE-ERIC Higher Education Report, 30*(3).

Gelman, A., and Hill, J. *Data Analysis Using Regression and Multilevel/Hierarchical Models.* New York: Cambridge University Press, 2007.

Goldstein, H. *Multilevel Statistical Models.* (3rd ed.). New York: Oxford University Press, 2003.

Halpin, R. "An Application of the Tinto Model to the Analysis of Freshman Persistence in a Community." *Community College Review,* 1990, *17,* 22–32.

Hox, J. *Multilevel Analysis: Techniques and Applications.* Mahwah, NJ: Lawrence Erlbaum Associates, 2002.

Hurd, S. N., and Stein, R. F. (eds.). *Building and Sustaining Learning Communities: The Syracuse University Experience.* Boston: Anker, 2004.

Kellogg, K. *Learning Communities.* Washington, DC: ERIC Clearinghouse on Higher Education, 1999. (ED430512).

Kinzie, J., and others. "The Relationship between Gender and Student Engagement in College." Paper presented at the Annual Meeting of the Association for the Study of Higher Education, 2007. Retrieved August 8, 2011, from http://citeseerx.ist.psu.edu/viewdoc/download?doi=10.1.1.169.6002&rep=rep1&type=pdf.

Kreft, I., and de Leeuw, J. *Introducing Multilevel Modeling.* Thousand Oaks, Calif.: Sage Publications, 1998.

Laufgraben, J. L., and Shapiro, N. S. *Sustaining and Improving Learning Communities.* San Francisco: Jossey-Bass, 2004.

Lee, J., Donlan, W., and Brown, E. F. "American Indian/Alaskan Native Undergraduate Retention at Predominantly White Institutions: An Elaboration of Tinto's Theory of College Student Departure." *Journal of College Student Retention: Research, Theory, and Practice,* 2010, *12,* 257–276.

Luke, D. A. *Multilevel Modeling*. Thousand Oaks, Calif.: Sage Publications, 2004.

Moulton, B. R. "Random Group Effects and the Precision of Regression Estimates." *Journal of Econometrics*, 1986, *32*(3), 385–397.

Pascarella, E. T., and Terenzini, P. T. *How College Affects Students: A Third Decade Of Research*. San Francisco: Jossey-Bass, 2005.

Pike, G. R. "Measuring QUALITY: A Comparison of U.S. News Rankings and NSSE Benchmarks." *Research in Higher Education*, 2004, *45*(2), 193–208.

Porter, S. "What Can Multilevel Models Add to Institutional Research?" In M. A. Coughlin (ed.), *Applications of Intermediate/Advanced Statistics in Institutional Research*. Tallahassee, Fla.: Association for Institutional Research, 2005.

Raudenbush, S. W., and Bryk, A. S. *Hierarchical Linear Models: Applications and Data Analysis Methods*. (2nd ed.). Thousand Oaks, Calif.: Sage Publications, 2002.

Schall, R. "Estimation in Generalized Linear Models with Random Effects." *Biometrika*, 1991, *78*(4), 719–727.

Shapiro, N. S., and Levine, J. H. *Creating Learning Communities: A Practical Guide to Winning Support, Organizing for Change, and Implementing Programs*. San Francisco: Jossey-Bass, 1999.

Smith, B. L. "The Challenge of Learning Communities as a Growing National Movement." Paper presented at the Association of American Colleges and Universities Conference on Learning Communities, Providence, R.I., 2001. Retrieved August 4, 2011, from http://www.cgc.maricopa.edu/academic-affairs/learn-comm/Learning%20Community%20References/The%20Challenge%20of%20Learning%20Communities%20as%20a%20Growing%20National%20Movement.pdf.

Smith, B. L., MacGregor, J., Matthews, R. S., and Gabelnick, F. *Learning Communities: Reforming Undergraduate Education*. San Francisco: Jossey-Bass, 2004.

Snijders, T.A.B., and Bosker, R. J. *Multilevel Analysis: An Introduction to Basic and Advanced Multilevel Modeling*. Thousand Oaks, Calif.: Sage Publications, 1999.

Soldner, L., Lee, Y., and Duby, P. "Welcome to the Block: Developing Freshman Learning Communities That Work." *Journal of College Student Retention*, 1999, *1*(2), 115–129.

Tabachnick, B. G., and Fidell, L. S. *Using Multivariate Statistics*. (5th ed.). Boston: Pearson, 2007.

Terenzini, P. T., and Pascarella, E. T. "Toward the Validation of Tinto's Model of College Student Attrition: A Review of Recent Studies." *Research in Higher Education*, 1980, *12*(3), 271–282.

Tinto, V. "Taking Student Retention Seriously: Rethinking the First Year of College." *NACADA Journal*, 1999, *19*(2), 5–10.

Tinto, V. *Learning Better Together: The Impact of Learning Communities on Student Success* (Higher Education Monograph Series 2003–1), 2003. Retrieved August 4, 2011, from http://www.nhcuc.org/pdfs/Learning_Better_Together.pdf.

Zhao, C. M., and Kuh, G. D. "Adding Value: Learning Communities and Student Engagement." *Research in Higher Education*, 2004, *45*(2), 115–138.

PU-SHIH DANIEL CHEN *is an assistant professor in the Department of Counseling and Higher Education at the University of North Texas.*

KRISTINA CRAGG *is associate vice president of institutional research at Bridgepoint Education.*

7

Multilevel modeling provides several advantages over traditional ordinary least squares regression analysis; however, reporting results to stakeholders can be challenging. This chapter identifies some useful principles for reporting results.

Multilevel Modeling: Presenting and Publishing the Results for Internal and External Constituents

Gary R. Pike, Louis M. Rocconi

Institutional researchers and higher education scholars are frequently confronted with hierarchical data in which students (or faculty) are nested within courses, academic disciplines, and institutions. For example, researchers using data sets from the National Center for Education Statistics (NCES), such as the National Education Longitudinal Study (NELS) or the National Postsecondary Student Aid Study (NPSAS), must deal with complex cluster-sampling designs in which students are nested within schools or colleges. Likewise, national surveys, such as the Cooperative Institutional Research Program (CIRP) or the National Survey of Student Engagement (NSSE), produce data sets in which students are nested within institutions. Even institutional researchers conducting single-institution analyses may be faced with data in which students or faculty members are nested within courses or academic disciplines.

Despite the prevalence of nested data in higher education, much of the research has failed to account adequately for the hierarchical nature of these data (Burstein, 1980a; Pascarella and Terenzini, 1991, 2005; Raudenbush and Bryk, 2002). An important reason nesting is too often ignored in higher education research is that traditional ordinary least squares (OLS) procedures require that researchers select a single level of analysis (for example, student, department, or institutions). If students are the unit of analysis, department and institutional characteristics must be disaggregated. If the institution is the unit of analysis, student and department characteristics must be aggregated. The conceptual and methodological problems that plague both approaches, including aggregation bias, misestimation of standard errors, and heterogeneity of regressions, have been well documented (Burstein, 1980a; Ethington, 1997; Raudenbush and Bryk, 2002).

Multilevel models provide an answer to the unit of analysis problem because these models allow researchers to simultaneously consider multiple levels of effects. As a result, many researchers are turning to this statistical approach (Smart, 2005). The appropriateness of hierarchical or multilevel modeling is evident in a recent study by Rocconi (2010). Using data from more than 50,000 students participating in NSSE 2006, he compared results produced by the hierarchical linear modeling (HLM) computer program (Raudenbush and others, 2004) to OLS regression results for models in which students and institutions were the units of analysis. Rocconi concluded that when higher education researchers are interested in accurately portraying institutional effects, they should utilize multilevel models.

The advantages provided by the statistical sophistication of multilevel modeling come at a price. The sophistication of the statistical techniques can make it more difficult to explain results, particularly to institutional decision makers and higher education policy makers. The goal of this chapter is to suggest some strategies for presenting complex, multilevel data and statistical results to institutional and higher education decision makers. The remainder of the chapter is organized around two examples. The first example uses multilevel modeling to evaluate the importance of the sending high school in models of predicted first-year grades that can be used to guide admission decisions, and the focus is on how results can be reported to institutional decision makers. The second example examines the effects of student characteristics and academic disciplines on self-reports of critical thinking. The focus in this example is on how researchers or a national survey organization might present results showing the complex, contingent effects of student engagement and academic major on critical thinking outcomes.

Example 1: Predicting First-Year Grades

The first example is taken from research published by Pike and Saupe (2002). The focus of the original study was on the possible benefits of using HLM, rather than OLS regression, to predict students' first-year grade point averages (GPAs). Although the results of the original study were equivocal regarding the superiority of HLM, they provide an opportunity to describe how the findings can be presented to campus leaders.

Background. Research has consistently found that first-year grades and other measures of success in college are related to students' scores on standardized tests (for example, ACT Assessment and SAT) and their performance in high school (Mathiasen, 1984; Mouw and Khanna, 1993; Willingham, 1985; Noble and Sawyer, 1987, 1997; Cabrera, Nora, and Castañeda, 1993). Several of these studies also concluded that standardized test scores and high school performance can be used to make college admission decisions (Willingham, 1985; Noble and Sawyer, 1987, 1997). Predictors of student success in college are not limited to student characteristics. Research on effective schools found that high school characteristics can have a significant effect on student success in college (Lee, Bryk, and Smith, 1993). Likewise, Adelman's (1999) analysis of High School and Beyond data revealed that the high school curriculum exerted a more powerful influence on success in college than either high school grades or test scores.

Given the potentially important role played by the sending high school, it is not surprising that several early studies included high schools as a variable in OLS regression analyses designed to predict first-year grades in college (Bloom and Peters, 1961; Tucker, 1963; Creaser, 1965). There are, however, several important limitations to these OLS regression models. Foremost among these is the misestimation of standard errors due to the nesting of students within high schools (Ethington, 1997). Burstein (1980a, 1980b) also noted that the OLS models may accurately predict first-year grades for students in general but provide poor estimates of grades for a specific high school. This can be a serious limitation when grades are used to make college admission decisions.

In their original study, Pike and Saupe (2002) analyzed data for 8,674 first-time college students from 124 high schools who enrolled at a midwestern university (MU) during the fall semesters between 1996 and 1999. Data from students enrolling during the first three fall semesters were used to estimate the multilevel prediction model, and the accuracy of the model was evaluated using data from the fall 1999 entering cohort. The dependent variable in all analyses was first-year GPA. Three student-level variables were included in the analysis: ACT Assessment composite score, high school class percentile rank, and whether the students had (1) or had not (0) met new core course requirements implemented in 1997. This last measure was included to assess the appropriateness of the new course requirements. Slightly less than 40 percent of the students who enrolled in fall 1996 did not meet the course requirements, whereas less than 10 percent of the enrolled students failed to meet the course requirements from fall 1997 to fall 1999.

Four school-level variables were included in the analysis. The first, school size, was represented by the mean of the number of students graduating from a high school each year from 1996 to 1998. School-average ability was represented by the mean ACT score of students from a high school, and attendance at MU was represented by the mean proportion of students in a high school graduating class that entered the university from

1996 to 1998. Control was represented by a dichotomous variable indicating whether the high school was private (1) or public (0).

Following procedures suggested by Ethington (1997), three models were specified and tested. The first model included an intercept at the student level and was analogous to a one-way analysis of variance in which high school was the independent variable. Results indicated there was statistically significant variation in the intercepts, accounting for 2.5 percent of the variance in first-year GPA. The second model included the three student-level variables. Both ACT score and high school percentile rank were centered about the grand means for all students. All three student-level variables were significantly related to first-year GPA and accounted for slightly more than 40 percent of the variance in GPA. The third model included the four high school measures, as level-two variables intended to explain variations in level-one intercepts across high schools. All of the measures, except public or private control, were centered about their grand means. Three of the measures were significantly related to variation in the level-one intercepts, but the coefficient for size of the sending high school was not statistically significant, and including this variable did not improve the predictive power of the model. The variable was dropped from the analysis and the model was reestimated. Results for the final model revealed that all level-one and level-two coefficients were statistically significant, and that the level-two variable accounted for slightly more than 36 percent of the variance in the intercepts. Table 7.1 presents the coefficients reported by Pike and Saupe (2002) for the final model.

Reporting Results. In addition to publishing the results of this research, findings were presented to the university's provost, vice chancellor for student affairs, and members of the enrollment management team. Although the audience consisted of intelligent, well-educated administrators, they were not experts in statistics or institutional research. Three principles guided efforts to make the study's findings accessible to institutional decision makers.

Table 7.1. Effects of Student and High School Characteristics on First-Year GPA

Student/High School Characteristic	Coefficient
Intercept	2.665*
Mean ACT for High School	0.062*
Percent Attending from High School	0.016*
Public/Private Control	0.125*
ACT Composite Score for Student	0.026*
Student's High School Class Percentile Rank	0.027*
Student Met Core Course Requirement	0.100*

*$p < 0.05$.
Source: Adapted from Table 3 in Pike and Saupe (2002), p. 198. Used with kind permission from Springer Science and Business Media B.V.

First, results were presented at a very general level and couched in the conclusions from previous research and practice. For example, rather than reporting that the coefficient representing the relationship between students' ACT Assessment composite scores and first-year college GPAs was 0.026, it was noted that there was a statistically significant positive relationship between ACT scores and grades. The presentation also included a reference to a previous study that found similar results. Likewise, it was reported that high school class percentile rank was positively related to first-year GPA and that the relationship was stronger than the relationship between ACT Assessment scores and GPA. Again, this finding was consistent with previous studies. Findings related to core course requirements being met provided an opportunity to discuss the appropriateness of the new admission requirements implemented in 1997. It was noted that the significant positive relationship between having met the new core course requirements and first-year GPA was clear evidence of the appropriateness of the new admission requirements.

A similar approach was followed in explaining the effects of high school characteristics. Instead of reporting coefficients, it was noted that measures of the average ability of students from a high school were positively related to first-year grades. It was explained that this finding was consistent with research showing that students from high-performing schools tend to be more successful in college. It was also noted that the significant positive relationship between the proportion of students from a high school that attended the university and first-year GPA was consistent with research on the success of students from "feeder" high schools. The positive relationship between attending a private high school and grades in college was also consistent with national research. Explaining these results, no doubt, was made easier by the fact that the findings were consistent with institutional leaders' experiences and perceptions.

The second approach used to explain the study's findings was to provide concrete examples of differences in predicted GPA based on student and high school differences. For example, it was noted that the predicted GPA of an average student who had met core course requirements was 2.76, whereas the predicted GPA of a student with an ACT Assessment score approximately 1 standard deviation (4 points) higher was 2.87. The same "average" student would have a predicted GPA of 3.03 if his or her class rank were 10 percentage points higher than average. This approach provided a convenient way to describe the unique effect of each student-level variable in the model after controlling for other student characteristics.

In presenting the results for high school characteristics, the actual characteristics of different high schools were utilized. Again, the "average" student who had met the core course admission requirements would be expected to have a predicted GPA of 2.76. It was explained that the same student from a major public feeder high school in the same city as the university would have a predicted GPA of 2.98. The higher predicted GPA was attributed to the fact that the average ACT score from the feeder high school was approximately 1 point higher than the average for all high schools, and the percentage of students attending the university from that high school was slightly less than 10 percentage points higher. A second example used in describing the results involved an elite private institution in a major metropolitan area within the state. The mean ACT composite score for students from that institution was nearly 3 points higher, the percentage of students from the high school attending the university was the same as the average for all high schools, and the high school was private. The predicted GPA for an "average" student from that institution was approximately 3.08. Again, the familiarity of leaders with the exemplar institutions made presentation of the HLM results more meaningful.

The third strategy used to present the results of the multilevel analysis was to compare the predictive accuracy of the HLM results with the results for the traditional OLS regression with no high school characteristics. Comparisons with the OLS model that included high schools as a series of dummy-coded variables were not shared with decision makers because this model was not considered to be practical for admission decisions. The classification results from the original study are summarized in Table 7.2. As can be seen from the results in the table, the hierarchical model that included high school characteristics was more accurate in identifying students who were likely to have less than a 2.00 first-year GPA (0.342 versus 0.231), slightly less accurate in identifying students with GPAs between 2.00 and 3.24 (0.827 compared to 0.864), and more accurate in identifying students with GPAs of 3.25 or higher (0.377 compared to 0.319). These results were very effective in underscoring the superiority of the multilevel model because students with first-year GPAs of less than 2.00 had very low persistence rates, and a first-year GPA of 3.25 was the cutoff for scholarship renewal.

Ultimately, the decision was made not to include characteristics of sending high schools in admission decisions because of the serious negative public relations that could result from the university being perceived to be favoring certain high schools over others. However, results from the multilevel modeling were used informally to help identify at-risk students (for instance, those students likely to have first-year GPAs below 2.00) and to assist in awarding scholarships in some borderline situations.

Table 7.2. Proportion of Correct Classifications in the Fall 1999 Cohort

	0.00–1.99	2.00–3.24	3.25–4.00
Traditional OLS	0.231	0.864	0.319
Hierarchical Model	0.342	0.827	0.377

Source: Adapted from Table 4 in Pike and Saupe (2002), p. 199. Used with kind permission from Springer Science and Business Media B.V.

Example 2: Critical Thinking Outcomes and Academic Disciplines

The second example demonstrates how an institution or a national survey organization might use multilevel modeling to examine the effects of student engagement on critical thinking ability and examine whether academic major influences students' critical thinking ability. Critical thinking is one of many desirable learning outcomes of postsecondary education, and exposure to higher education is often linked with higher levels of critical thinking (Facione, 1997; Pascarella and Terenzini, 2005). There is substantial evidence that the development of critical thinking skills is related to student engagement (Kuh and Hu, 1999; Whitt and others, 1999; Carini, Kuh, and Klein, 2006). Moreover, there is evidence to suggest that students' academic major affects critical thinking (Pascarella and Terenzini, 1991, 2005; Smart, Feldman, and Ethington, 2000).

Background. The following example uses data from the 2006 administration of the NSSE. Only senior students who began college at their current institution were selected for the sample. The restriction to include only senior students who began at their current institution was made to maximize the likely impact of academic major on critical thinking outcomes. The final sample used in this example consists of 56,276 senior students in 58 majors from 405 United States institutions who had complete data on all variables used in the analysis. For the purposes of this illustration, institutional characteristics are not included in the model.

The dependent variable used in the analyses is a scale representing students' perceptions of their gains in critical thinking abilities. The NSSE survey asked students questions regarding the extent to which their experiences at their current institution contributed to their knowledge, skills, and personal development in thinking critically and analytically, analyzing quantitative problems, and solving complex real-world problems. The alpha reliability coefficient for perceived gains in critical thinking ability was 0.79. The level-one predictors of critical thinking ability are three scales representing students' exposure to higher-order thinking in coursework, students' academic effort, and student–faculty interaction. The six items in the higher-order thinking (HOT) skills scale asked students the extent to which their coursework emphasized analyzing and synthesizing ideas, making judgments, and applying theories. The 11 items making up the academic effort (AE) scale asked students questions related to course rigor and preparation. The five items of the student–faculty interaction (SFI) scale asked students about discussions and interactions with faculty members. All scales were created by summing across the items. Each summed score was then converted to a T-score. Alpha reliability coefficients for these scales are 0.80, 0.67, and 0.77, respectively.

The characteristics of academic majors that were hypothesized to influence critical thinking were Biglan's (1973a, 1973b) hard versus soft dimension and pure versus applied dimension. The hard versus soft dimension (HARD) reflects the degree to which an academic discipline possesses a clearly delineated paradigm. The pure versus applied dimension (PURE) reflects the academic discipline's concern with practical application. Each major was classified as either hard or soft and either pure or applied based on results reported by Biglan (1973a, 1973b). For example, mathematics was classified as both "Hard" and "Pure" whereas finance was classified as both "Soft" and "Applied." The hard versus soft dimension was coded 0 for soft disciplines and 1 for hard disciplines. The pure versus applied dimension was coded 0 for applied disciplines and 1 for pure disciplines.

Because the focus of this example was on the effects of student engagement and academic discipline on critical thinking, it was decided to keep the model simple and estimate a random intercept-only model. Thus, all slope effects were specified as fixed. The model to be estimated was:

$$CT_{ij} = \beta_{0j} + \beta_{1j}(HOT) + \beta_{2j}(AE) + \beta_{3j}(SFI) + r_{ij}$$

$$\beta_{0j} = \gamma_{00} + \gamma_{01}(HARD) + \gamma_{02}(SOFT) + u_{0j}$$

The first step in the HLM analysis was estimating a base model with no level-one or level-two predictor. The purpose was to model student-level variance in critical thinking as a function of variability within majors (or among students) and variability due to between-major differences. In this case, the proportion of variance between majors was slightly less than 5 percent and the proportion of variance among students was 95 percent. A chi-square test ($\chi^2 = 2208.07$, $df = 57$, $p < .001$) indicated that critical thinking scores varied significantly between majors. Decomposition of the variability in critical thinking indicated that, by far, the more important sources of variability were those associated with characteristics of individual students. That is, differences in students' perceived critical thinking ability was to a far greater extent the result of individual differences than it was due to differences in majors.

The second step in the analysis required estimating a model that included the three student-level variables. All three variables were centered around their respective group means. The practical result of group-mean centering was that the intercept for each academic discipline represented the critical thinking score of a student whose engagement scores were at the mean for that discipline. All three student engagement variables were significantly related to critical thinking ability and accounted for slightly more than 30 percent of the variance in critical thinking ability. In the final step, the two characteristics of academic majors (HARD and PURE) were added to the model and were intended to explain variations in level-one intercepts across majors. Both level-two variables were entered into the model uncentered. Results for the final model revealed that all level-one and level-two coefficients were statistically significant and that the level-two variables accounted for 47 percent of the variance in the intercepts. Table 7.3 presents the results for the final model.

Reporting Results. Again, several general principles can be helpful in reporting the findings of this research to institutional leaders and higher education policy makers. The first principle is to present the results at a very general level and compare results to previous research. Instead of reporting that the coefficient representing the relationship between higher-order thinking skills and students' perceived critical thinking ability was 0.391, it was noted that there was a statistically significant positive relationship between higher-order thinking skills and critical thinking ability. Call attention to the fact that students who reported that their coursework emphasized higher-order thinking skills also reported greater critical thinking ability. Likewise, students who reported greater levels of academic effort also reported greater levels of critical thinking. The same can be said regarding the effect of student–faculty interaction; students who reported more frequent interactions with faculty members also reported higher levels of critical thinking ability. Also, be sure to include appropriate references to previous studies that found similar results between student engagement and critical thinking.

A similar approach can be followed for reporting the effects of the major characteristics. Instead of reporting the coefficients, it can be

Table 3. Effects of Student Engagement and Academic Disciplines on Critical Thinking

Fixed Effects	Coefficient	S.E.	t-Ratio	Reliability
Intercept	49.92	0.288	173.36*	0.924
Level 1: Effects on student critical thinking				
Higher-Order Thinking Skills	0.391	0.007	58.43*	
Academic Effort	0.137	0.006	23.18*	
Student–Faculty Interaction	0.123	0.007	18.27*	
Level 2: Effects on average critical thinking across majors				
HARD	2.753	0.479	5.75*	
PURE	−1.800	0.449	−4.01*	

Random Effects	Variance	DF	Chi-Square	
σ^2: variance among students within majors	66.587			
τ^π: variance among majors within institutions	2.663	55	1714.84*	

*$p < .001$.

noted that students majoring in hard disciplines, such as biology and mathematics, tend to perceive they have made greater gains in critical thinking abilities than students in soft disciplines, such as economics and art. In addition, students majoring in applied fields, such as accounting and nursing, tend to perceive greater gains in critical thinking abilities than students majoring in pure disciplines, such as geography and sociology.

A second principle to emerge from these analyses is that it can be helpful to discuss the relative impact of exposure to higher-order thinking, academic effort, and student–faculty interaction on critical thinking ability. Because all three level-one variables were converted to T-scores, we can tell that higher-order thinking skills had the strongest effect on critical thinking ability. Moreover, the impact of higher-order thinking skills on critical thinking was twice as large as the effects of academic effort and student–faculty interaction. This finding provides an opportunity to discuss with faculty and administrators ways to increase students' exposure to higher-order thinking in the classroom. It could be noted that, because higher-order thinking skills has the strongest impact on critical thinking, institutions interested in increasing students' critical thinking abilities could focus their efforts on interventions that promote higher-order thinking skills.

A third principle for reporting results is to use charts and graphs to explain complex results. In this example, the use of graphs to explain the impact of the characteristics of academic majors on critical thinking was very effective. Graphs can be produced easily in the HLM computer program. Figure 7.1 is a bar graph produced by HLM that shows the impact of the two characteristics of academic majors (HARD and PURE) on students' perceived critical thinking ability. The graph clearly displays differences in the average critical thinking ability reported by students in each of the four discipline categories (Hard/Pure, Hard/Applied, Soft/Pure, Soft/Applied). From the graph we see that students in Hard/Applied disciplines, such as engineering or medicine, report the highest levels of critical thinking ability, and students in Soft/Pure disciplines report the lowest levels of critical thinking ability. This graph gives a good visual display that students in hard disciplines, regardless of whether they are in Hard/Pure or Hard/Applied disciplines, tend to report greater critical thinking ability than students in soft disciplines.

Principles of Effective Reporting

Four general principles of effective reporting emerged from the two examples we presented. First and foremost, keep the results simple, or at least nontechnical, and couch the results in terms of previous research and practice. In efforts to predict first-year grades using multilevel models, reporting focused on the fact that the results were statistically significant and that the directions of the relationships between first-year GPA and

NEW DIRECTIONS FOR INSTITUTIONAL RESEARCH • DOI: 10.1002/ir

Figure 7.1. Effects of Major Characteristics on Critical Thinking

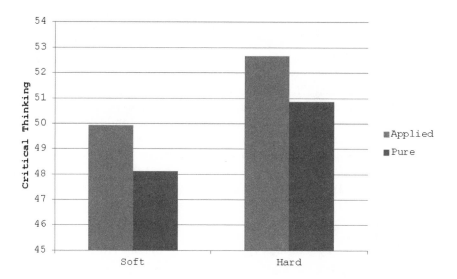

both high school grades and test scores were positive. Explaining the findings in the context of previous research and institutional practice also made the results more meaningful to campus decision makers.

The same principle was applied when reporting findings regarding the relationships between student engagement measures and gains in critical thinking. In the second example, all of the student engagement measures were on the same measurement scale (T-scores). This allowed the relative strength of the relationships to be easily compared and provided an effective vehicle for generating discussions about what could be done to improve students' critical thinking abilities. In the first example, test scores and grades were not on the same measurement scales, and comparisons of the relative effects of the student-level variables had to rely on the use of concrete examples.

The use of concrete examples in reporting the results of multilevel models was a second principle to emerge from the examples provided. As just noted, the use of concrete examples allowed a comparison of the relative importance of test scores, high school grades, and core course admission standards to students' grades during the first year of college. The use of concrete examples also provided an opportunity to present the results for high school characteristics to campus decision makers who were familiar with archetypical high schools that represented the variables in the level-two model. It was more difficult to apply this principle to the study of academic disciplines and critical thinking outcomes. Although it would have been possible to use specific disciplines (for example, math, biology,

English, or history) to describe the level-two results, the fact that the level-two variables were dichotomous made this a less effective approach than the use of graphs.

The third principle to emerge from the examples presented here is that visual presentation of results can be very effective. The graph presented in Figure 7.1 shows how results can be communicated clearly and simply. The fact that both characteristics of academic majors were dichotomous variables made it possible to present results as simple bar graphs. When explanatory variables are continuous, line graphs can be used to depict the effects of the level-two variables. Exploring the effects of interactions among variables (for example, a comparison of hard/pure disciplines to soft/applied disciplines) is more difficult using line graphs of continuous variables.

The fourth principle of reporting to emerge from these examples is that examining the predictive accuracy of a model can be an effective method of reporting results. However, this approach is appropriate only when prediction is an objective of the analysis. In the first example, prediction of college students' first-year grades was the objective of the study, and the predictive accuracy of the hierarchical model was an important consideration. When predictive accuracy is used as a criterion for evaluating a model, it is important to select classifications that have meaning to decision makers. In the case of predicting first-year grades, accuracy in predicting at-risk students (less than a 2.00 GPA) and predicting scholarship renewal (a GPA of 3.25 or greater) were classifications that were relevant to campus decision makers and greatly assisted in effectively communicating the results of the analyses.

Taken together, these four principles of effective reporting suggest an even more general principle for reporting the results of multilevel modeling: researchers should first determine what types of understanding and action they are seeking from decision makers and then communicate results in a manner that is most likely to yield the desired understanding and action.

References

Adelman, C. *Answers in the Tool Box: Academic Intensity, Attendance Patterns, and Bachelor's Degree Attainment.* Washington, D.C.: U.S. Government Printing Office, 1999.

Biglan, A. "The Characteristics of Subject Matter in Different Academic Areas." *Journal of Applied Psychology,* 1973a, 57(3), 195–203.

Biglan, A. "Relationships Between Subject Matter Characteristics and the Structure and Output of University Departments." *Journal of Applied Psychology,* 1973b, 57(3), 204–213.

Bloom, B. S., and Peters, F. R. *The Use of Academic Prediction Scales for Counseling and Selecting College Entrants.* New York: The Free Press of Glencoe, 1961.

Burstein, L. "The Analysis of Multilevel Data in Educational Research and Evaluation." In D. C. Berliner (ed.), *Review of Research in Education,* Vol. 8. Washington, D.C.: American Educational Research Association, 1980a.

Burstein, L. "The Role of Levels of Analysis in the Specification of Education Effects." In R. Dreeben and J. A. Thomas (eds.), *The Analysis of Educational Productivity, Vol. I: Issues in microanalysis.* Cambridge, Mass.: Ballinger, 1980b.

Cabrera, A. F., Nora, A., and Castañeda, M. B. "College Persistence: Structural Modeling of an Integrated Model of Student Retention." *Journal of Higher Education,* 1993, 64(2), 123–139.

Carini, R. M., Kuh, G. D., and Klein, S. P. "Student Engagement and Student Learning: Testing the Linkages." *Research in Higher Education,* 2006, 47(1), 1–32.

Creaser, J. W. "Predicting College Success from Equated High School Ranks: A Cross-Validation Study." *College and University,* 1965, 41, 96–100.

Ethington, C. A. "A Hierarchical Linear Modeling Approach to Studying College Effects." In J. C. Smart (ed.), *Higher Education: Handbook of Theory and Research.* Vol. 12. New York: Agathon Press, 1997.

Facione, N. *Critical Thinking Assessment in Nursing Education Programs: An Aggregate Data Analysis.* Millbrae, Calif.: California Academic Press, 1997.

Kuh, G. D., and Hu, S. "Is More Better? Student-Faculty Interaction Revisited." Paper presented at the Association for the Study of Higher Education, San Antonio, Texas, 1999.

Lee, V. E., Bryk, A. S., and Smith, J. B. "The Organization of Effective Secondary Schools." In L. Darling-Hammond (ed.), *Review of Research in Education,* Vol. 19. Washington, D.C.: American Educational Research Association, 1993.

Mathiasen, R. L. "Predicting College Academic Achievement: A Research Review." *College Student Journal,* 1984, 18(4), 380–386.

Mouw, J., and Khanna, R. "Prediction of Academic Success: A Review of the Literature and Some Recommendations." *College Student Journal,* 1993, 27(3), 328–336.

Noble, J., and Sawyer, R. *Predicting Grades in Specific College Freshman Courses from ACT Test Scores and Self-Reported High School Grades.* ACT Research Report Series, 87–20. Iowa City: American College Testing Program, 1987.

Noble, J., and Sawyer, R. "Alternative Methods for Validating Admission and Course Placement Criteria." *AIR Professional File,* 1997, No. 63, 1–9.

Pascarella, E., and Terenzini, P. *How College Affects Students: Findings and Insights from Twenty Years of Research.* San Francisco: Jossey-Bass, 1991.

Pascarella, E., and Terenzini, P. *How College Affects Students: A Third Decade of Research.* San Francisco: Jossey-Bass, 2005.

Pike, G. R., and Saupe, J. L. "Does High School Matter? An Analysis of Three Methods of Predicting First-Year Grades." *Research in Higher Education,* 2002, 43(2), 187–207.

Raudenbush, S. W., and Bryk, A. S. *Hierarchical Linear Models: Applications and Data Analysis Methods.* (2nd ed.). Thousand Oaks, Calif.: Sage Publications, 2002.

Raudenbush, S. W., and others. *HLM 6: Hierarchical Linear and Nonlinear Modeling.* Chicago: Scientific Software International, 2004.

Rocconi, L. M. "Analyzing Multilevel Data: An Empirical Comparison of Parameter Estimates of Hierarchical Linear Modeling and Ordinary Least Squares Regression." Unpublished doctoral dissertation, University of Memphis, 2010.

Smart, J. C. "Perspectives of the Editor: Attributes of Exemplary Research Manuscripts Employing Quantitative Analyses." *Research in Higher Education,* 2005, 46(4), 461–477.

Smart, J. C., Feldman, K. A., and Ethington, C. A. *Academic disciplines: Holland's Theory and the Study of College Students and Faculty.* Nashville, Tenn.: Vanderbilt University Press, 2000.

Tucker, L. R. *Formal Models for a Central Prediction System* (Psychometric Monograph no. 10). Richmond, Va.: William Byrd Press, 1963.

Whitt, E., and others. "Interaction with Peers and Objective and Self-Reported Cognitive Outcomes across Three Years of College." *Journal of College Student Development*, 1999, *40*(1), 61–78.

Willingham, W. *Success in College: The Role of Personal Qualities and Academic Ability.* New York: College Board, 1985.

GARY R. PIKE is the executive director of information management and institutional research at Indiana University-Purdue University-Indianapolis and associate professor of higher education and student affairs at Indiana University.

LOUIS M. ROCCONI is an assistant research scientist with the Center for Postsecondary Research at Indiana University.

NEW DIRECTIONS FOR INSTITUTIONAL RESEARCH • DOI: 10.1002/ir

INDEX

ACT scores, 113, 114t, 115

Adelman, C., 113

African American students: using multi-level models to study how to increase enrollment of, 11–18; student learning outcome study sample of, 99–100t, 105t

Agresti, A., 57, 62

AIC (Akaike Information Criterion), 32–34

Aiken, L. S., 36

Alig, J. L., 10

Allison, P. D., 64

American Association of University Professors, 78

American Indian/Alaskan Native students: using multilevel models to study how to increase enrollment of, 11–18; student learning outcome study sample of, 99–100t, 105t

American Statistical Association, 8

Anderson, D. R., 32

ANOVA model: HLM one-way, 102–103; one-way analysis of variance, 101

Applications of Intermediate/Advanced Statistics in Institutional Research (Porter), 96

Asian American students: using multi-level models to study how to increase enrollment of, 11–18; student learning outcome study sample of, 99–100t, 105t

Astin, A. W., 2, 44

Baccalaureate and Beyond (B&B), 43t, 46

Barbezat, D., 78

Becker, W. E., 81

Beginning Postsecondary Students (BPS), 43t

Bellas, M. L., 78

Beretvas, S. N., 77, 78, 79

Berger, M.P.F., 18, 19

BIC (Bayesian Information Criterion), 32–34

Bickel, R., 96

Biesanz, J. C., 37

Biglan, A., 118

Binary (or binomial) data: modeling categorical outcomes of, 58; modeling postdoctoral placement, 64–67fig; modeling program dropout, 69–73fig, 74fig; models for clustered, 63–73fig, 74fig; multilevel models for categorical outcomes of, 60–62; overview of common models for, 58–60; range of data analysis models for, 57–58

Birkett, N., 7

Black, A. C., 23, 39

Blitstein, J. L., 19

Blood, E. A., 95

Bloom, B. S., 113

Bloom, H. S., 19

Booth, J. C., 62

Bosker, R., 2, 11, 27, 35, 61, 95

Bozdogan, H., 32, 33

Braxton, J. M., 99

Bringle, R. G., 44

Brittingham, B., 10

Brown, E. F., 107

Bryant, A. N., 44

Bryk, A. S., 1, 2, 8, 9, 11, 12, 16, 23, 24, 26, 26, 27, 28, 29, 34, 35, 38, 47, 48, 61, 62, 74, 77, 78, 81, 95, 101, 103, 104, 111, 112, 113

Buck, C., 7

Burnham, K. P., 32

Burstein, L., 111, 112, 113

Cabral, H., 95

Cabrera, A. F., 113

Caffo, B., 62

Carini, R. M., 117

Carnegie Classification System, 81

Carnegie Foundation for the Advancement of Teaching, 99

Castañeda, M. B., 113

Categorical data analysis: mapping z to the cumulative probability $F(z)$, 59fig; models for clustered binary data, 63–73fig, 74fig; multilevel models for, 60–62; overview of common models for binary and binomial responses, 58–60; range of methods and models for, 57–58

125

Field, A., 48
FIML (full information maximum-likelihood) estimation: deviance measured by using, 30–31; deviance measured using, 26–27
Fineberg, S. E., 57
First-year college students: comparing OLS regression with HLM for predicting grades of, 112–116t, 122; effects of student and high school characteristics on GPA of, 114t; factors that have an impact on GPA of, 107fig; learning communities to enrich experience of, 98; student learning outcomes study on, 98, 99–107fig
Fixed coefficients model, 64
Fixed effects: description of, 27–28; hypothesis testing in HLM program, 28–29
Florida Department of Education Student Database, 45
Foster, V., 36
Fowler, F. J., 7
Freshman Learning Community, 98
Freshman Survey, 43

Gabelnick, F., 97, 98, 99
Gardner, S., 69
Gelman, A., 7, 11, 36, 42, 50, 96
Gender differences: faculty gender pay study findings on, 79–91fig; student learning outcomes study findings on, 100–101
Gender pay equity. See Faculty gender pay study
Goldstein, H. I., 8, 9, 60, 61, 95
Goldstein, J., 11
GPA (grade point average): comparing OLS regression with HLM for predicting first-year, 112–116t, 122; effects of student and high school characteristics on first-year, 114t; factors that have an impact on first-year college, 107fig; student learning outcomes study findings on, 101–107; as student learning outcomes study variable, 99–101. See also Student success
Graham, J. W., 52
Greene, T. G., 45
Guo, G., 62

Hadfield, J. D., 50
Halpin, R., 98

Hannon, P. J., 7
Harper, C. E., 44
Hatcher, J. A., 44
Health Insurance Portability and Accountability Act (1996), 46
Heck, R. H., 42
Hedges, L. V., 19
Heeren, T., 95
HERI Faculty Survey, 43
Hernandez, J. M., 41, 55
Heuer, R., 81
Hierarchical linear modeling (HLM): advantages to institutional research (IR) by, 5–8, 47–48; comparing OLS results with, 112–120; of critical thinking outcomes and academic disciplines, 117–120, 121fig, 122; description of, 1, 47, 95; GUI (graphical user interface) of, 47–48; limitations of, 48; multiple imputation in, 52; nested data of, 2; predicting first-year GPA, 112–116t, 122; student learning outcomes study results from means-as-outcomes model of, 101, 103–104t. See also Multilevel modeling (MLM); Software programs
Hierarchical linear models: for data analysis of longitudinal data, 61–62; GLMM (generalized linear mixed model), 63
Hierarchical (or clustered) data, 61
High School and Beyond, 43t
Higher education institutions: Carnegie Classification System of, 81; faculty gender pay study on, 78–92; impact of learning communities on, 98–99; IR (institutional research) functions within, 1, 10–11; modeling post-doctoral placement of students in, 64–67fig; modeling program dropout of STEM students in, 69–73fig, 74fig. See also Students
Higher Education Research Institute (HERI), 43
Higher-order thinking (HOT) skills scale, 117
Hill, J., 7, 11, 42, 50, 96
Hirschy, A. S., 99
Hispanic students: using multilevel models to study how to increase enrollment of, 11–18; student learning outcome study sample of, 99–100t, 105t
Hobert, J. P., 62
Hox, J. J., 18, 61, 95

IR 150   Validity and Limitations of College Student Self-Report Data
          Serge Herzog, Nicholas A. Bowman
          Higher education administrators, institutional researchers (IR), and scholars
          rely heavily on the survey responses of college students, not least to meet
          mounting accountability pressures to document student learning and
          institutional effectiveness. However, research on the accuracy of students'
          self-reported learning, development, and experiences is quite limited. To
          address this critical issue, *Validity and Limitations of College Student Self-
          Report Data* provides seven empirical studies that examine the validity, use,
          and interpretation of such data, with an emphasis on student self-reported
          gains. The chapters are written by leading scholars in the field of college
          student self-reports, and they provide IR practitioners several analytical
          frameworks to gauge the accuracy of student survey data. The cumulative
          findings from this volume suggest that self-reported gains exhibit some
          significant biases, and they often do not constitute an adequate proxy for
          longitudinal measures of learning and development. Still, student self-
          reports offer important subjective impressions about learning and affective
          development that may complement direct measures of outcomes, together
          yielding a more comprehensive picture of the college experience.
          ISBN: 978-1-1181-3416-0

IR 149   Assessing Complex General Education Student Learning Outcomes
          Jeremy D. Penn
          One of the greatest challenges in assessing student learning in general
          education programs is addressing the tension between selecting easy-
          to-measure learning outcomes that have little value or bearing on our
          institutions' goals and selecting meaningful and substantial learning
          outcomes that are complex and difficult to assess. Many institutions that
          have recently replaced their cafeteria-style general education programs
          with general education programs that focus on complex student learning
          outcomes find themselves at a loss in attempting to gather evidence on
          student achievement of these outcomes for internal improvement and
          external accountability purposes.
               This volume of *New Directions for Institutional Research* makes a
          compelling case that institutions can and should be assessing consequential,
          complex general education student learning outcomes. It also gives faculty
          members and assessment leaders the tools and resources to take ownership
          of this important work. Part One of this volume provides an argument for
          why we should be assessing general education and describes a framework,
          based on a rigorous psychological research approach, for engaging in
          assessment. The six chapters in Part Two show how this work can be (and
          is being) done for six important learning outcomes: critical thinking,
          quantitative reasoning, teamwork, intercultural competence, civic knowledge
          and engagement, and integrative learning. The volume closes with
          recommendations on needed innovations in general education assessment
          and presents a research agenda for future work.
          ISBN: 978-1-1180-9133-3

IR 148   Students of Color in STEM
          Shaun R. Harper, Christopher B. Newman
          Why are some racial minorities so underrepresented as degree candidates in
          science, technology, engineering, and mathematics (STEM)? Why are they
          so underprepared for college-level math and science courses? Why are their
          grades and other achievement indicators disproportionately lower than their
          white counterparts? Why do so many of them change their majors to non-
          STEM fields? And why do so few pursue graduate degrees in STEM? These
          five questions are continuously recycled in the study of students of color in

STEM. Offered in this volume of *New Directions for Institutional Research* are new research ideas and frameworks that have emerged from recent studies of minorities in STEM fields across a wide array of institution types: large research universities, community colleges, minority-serving institutions, and others. The chapter authors counterbalance examinations of student underperformance and racial disparities in STEM with insights into the study of factors that enable minority student success.
ISBN: 978-1-1180-1402-8

IR 147   System Offices for Community College Institutional Research
Willard C. Hom
This volume of *New Directions for Institutional Research* examines a professional niche that tends to operate with a low profile while playing a major role in state policies—the system office for community college institutional research. As states, regions, and the federal government seek ways to evaluate and improve the performance of community colleges, this office has grown in importance. The chapter authors, all institutional researchers in this area, draw a timely state-of-the-niche portrait by showing how this office varies across states, how it varies from other institutional research offices within states, and the implications its history and prospects have for the future. This volume will be particularly useful for those who deal with higher education policy at the state, regional, or federal level; on-campus institutional researchers; and individuals who currently work in or with these system offices.
ISBN: 978-04709-39543

IR 146   Institutional Research and Homeland Security
Nicolas A. Valcik
Although homeland security has captured the public's attention in recent years, higher education institutions have had to contend with emergency situations and security issues long before 9/11 occurred. Well known incidents such as the Unabomber attacks and decades of sporadic school shootings brought violence to college campuses long before the Department of Homeland Security was established. Despite these past security issues and the passage of the PATRIOT Act, very little research has been performed on homeland security issues and higher education institutions. This volume of *New Directions for Institutional Research* examines how new federal regulations impact institutional research and higher education institutions. This volume also addresses key issues such as right-to-privacy regulations, criminal background checks, the Student and Exchange Visitor Information System (SEVIS), information technology security, the use of geographic information systems as a research tool, hazardous materials (HAZMAT) management, and the impact of natural disasters and manmade threats on applications and enrollment.
ISBN: 978-04709-03148

NEW DIRECTIONS FOR INSTITUTIONAL RESEARCH

ORDER FORM SUBSCRIPTION AND SINGLE ISSUES

DISCOUNTED BACK ISSUES:

Use this form to receive 20% off all back issues of *New Directions for Institutional Research*.
All single issues priced at **$23.20** (normally $29.00)

TITLE	ISSUE NO.	ISBN
_____	_____	_____
_____	_____	_____
_____	_____	_____

Call 888-378-2537 or see mailing instructions below. When calling, mention the promotional code JBNND to receive your discount. For a complete list of issues, please visit www.josseybass.com/go/ndir

SUBSCRIPTIONS: (1 YEAR, 4 ISSUES)

☐ New Order   ☐ Renewal

U.S.	☐ Individual: $109	☐ Institutional: $297
CANADA/MEXICO	☐ Individual: $109	☐ Institutional: $337
ALL OTHERS	☐ Individual: $133	☐ Institutional: $371

Call 888-378-2537 or see mailing and pricing instructions below.
Online subscriptions are available at www.onlinelibrary.wiley.com

ORDER TOTALS:

Issue / Subscription Amount: $ _____

Shipping Amount: $ _____
(for single issues only – subscription prices include shipping)

Total Amount: $ _____

SHIPPING CHARGES:

First Item $6.00
Each Add'l Item $2.00

(No sales tax for U.S. subscriptions. Canadian residents, add GST for subscription orders. Individual rate subscriptions must be paid by personal check or credit card. Individual rate subscriptions may not be resold as library copies.)

BILLING & SHIPPING INFORMATION:

☐ **PAYMENT ENCLOSED:** *(U.S. check or money order only. All payments must be in U.S. dollars.)*

☐ **CREDIT CARD:**   ☐ VISA   ☐ MC   ☐ AMEX

Card number _____Exp. Date_____

Card Holder Name_____Card Issue # _____

Signature _____Day Phone_____

☐ **BILL ME:** *(U.S. institutional orders only. Purchase order required.)*

Purchase order # _____
Federal Tax ID 13559302 • GST 89102-8052

Name_____

Address_____

Phone_____ E-mail_____

Copy or detach page and send to: **John Wiley & Sons, One Montgomery Street, Suite 1200, San Francisco, CA 94104-4594**

Order Form can also be faxed to: **888-481-2665**

PROMO JBNND